Packet Tracer Network Simulator

Simulate an unlimited number of devices
on a network using Packet Tracer

Jesin A

BIRMINGHAM - MUMBAI

Packet Tracer Network Simulator

First published: January 2014

Production Reference: 1100114

Published by Packt Publishing Ltd.
Livery Place
35 Livery Street
Birmingham B3 2PB, UK.

ISBN 978-1-78217-042-6

www.packtpub.com

Cover Image by Artie Ng (artherng@yahoo.com.au)

Credits

About the Author

Jesin A is a network security specialist with an immense interest in Linux and networking. He holds certificates in CCNP, RHCE, and CEH and also likes programming with PHP. He currently lives in Chennai and when he isn't securing networks, he enjoys computer gaming of the FPS genre. He holds a bachelor's degree in computer applications from Loyola College, Chennai.

I would like to thank Mohammad Rizvi (Author Relationship Executive) at Packt Publishing for providing me with this opportunity. I would also like to thank Meeta Rajani, Aboli Ambardekar, Mohammed Fahad, and the entire Packt editorial team for guiding me through this project.

About the Reviewers

Saumya Dwivedi is a B.Tech Computer Science final year student at IIT Hyderabad. While a student of Advanced Computer Networking, Saumya has undertaken and worked on Packet Simulator-related academic projects. She has also worked on ICMP security and packet capture, Responsive Web Design, and Ruby on Rails Web Applications.

John Herbert, CCIE® #6727 (Routing & Switching), has been moving packets around networks for over 15 years, and has been doing so as a consultant since 1999. In his spare time, he blogs at `http://lamejournal.com/` and can be found on Twitter as `@mrtugs`. John lives in Atlanta, Georgia, with his wife and three children, and has a home network that is arguably the very definition of "overkill".

Samad Najjargabel is an M.Sc. student in Computer Engineering (Software) at the University of Tabriz. He received his B.Sc. in Computer Engineering (Software) from the University of Mohaghegh Ardabili in 2013. His main interests are Computer Networks, Network Security, Service Oriented Architecture (SOA), and developing and modeling software. His personal webpage is `www.samadnajjar.ir` and he can be contacted by e-mail at `samad.najjar@gmail.com`

Bhargesh Bharatbhai Patel completed his M.Tech in Computer Engineering at the Dharmsinh Desai University, Nadiad. He has more than two years of teaching experience in Cloud Computing and Networking. Currently, he is working with G H Patel College of Engineering & Technology, Vallabh Vidyanagar. His areas of interest are Cloud Computing, Grid Computing, Data mining, Operating systems, and Computer Networks.

Samia Yousif holds M.Sc and B.Sc degrees from the University of Bahrain, as well as CCNA, CCNP, and CCDA certificates from the Bahrain Training Institute. She has extensive knowledge of and has developed her skills in various technical fields of Computer Science and IT. She has prepared conference publications and books, and received an e-Government Excellence Award (e-Education Award). She has been selected for reviewing books published by Packt Publishing Pvt. Ltd. She has delivered several IT workshops and attended many seminars. Samia has eight years of teaching experience at the undergraduate level in CS and IT. Furthermore, she has worked on the development of numerous systems and professional website applications using the most up-to-date web technologies. She is now a Lecturer of Multimedia Science at the Ahlia University, Kingdom of Bahrain and is planning to undertake a Ph.D program.

For more details about Samia, please visit her website `http://samiayousif.hostoi.com`

Other books she has worked on are:

- *Object Oriented Techniques for an Intelligent Multi-Lingual Dictionary System, Samia Yousif* and *Mansoor Al-Aali, IGI Global (member of* `www.Amazon.com`*), U.S.A, December, 2013.*

- *Computer Jobs & Certifications: Choose & improve your IT career, Mansoor Al-Aali* and *Samia Yousif, Lulu (member of* `www.Amazon.com`*), U.S.A, August, 2012.*

- *HTML Fundamental, Samia Yousif, Royal University for Women, October, 2006.*

- *HTML Fundamental, Samia Yousif, AMA International University, Bahrain, May, 2006.*

www.PacktPub.com

Support files, eBooks, discount offers and more

You might want to visit www.PacktPub.com for support files and downloads related to your book.

Did you know that Packt offers eBook versions of every book published, with PDF and ePub files available? You can upgrade to the eBook version at www.PacktPub.com and as a print book customer, you are entitled to a discount on the eBook copy. Get in touch with us at service@packtpub.com for more details.

At www.PacktPub.com, you can also read a collection of free technical articles, sign up for a range of free newsletters and receive exclusive discounts and offers on Packt books and eBooks.

http://PacktLib.PacktPub.com

Do you need instant solutions to your IT questions? PacktLib is Packt's online digital book library. Here, you can access, read, and search across Packt's entire library of books.

Why subscribe?

- Fully searchable across every book published by Packt
- Copy and paste, print and bookmark content
- On demand and accessible via web browser

Free access for Packt account holders

If you have an account with Packt at www.PacktPub.com, you can use this to access PacktLib today and view nine entirely free books. Simply use your login credentials for immediate access.

Instant updates on new Packt books

Get notified! Find out when new books are published by following @PacktEnterprise on Twitter, or the *Packt Enterprise* Facebook page.

Table of Contents

Preface

Cisco Packet Tracer is a network simulator that can be used not just by students but also by instructors and network administrators. This software provides a wide range of Cisco switches and routers running on IOS 12 and IOS 15, wireless devices from Linksys, and several end devices such as PCs and servers with a command line. It is more than just a simulator and provides physical simulation as well as an assessment tool. The assessment tool can be used to create practical networking questions with a complex scoring model. The physical workspace provided can be used to determine the range of wireless devices.

This book serves as a guide to those using Packet Tracer, be it students, instructors, or administrators. This book differs from others by providing more information on the how-tos of Packet Tracer rather than computer networking. You'll learn how to efficiently use Packet Tracer to learn and understand packet flows in a topology.

What this book covers

Chapter 1, Getting Started with Packet Tracer, starts with a short introduction of Packet Tracer, protocols supported by it, and explains its installation on Windows and Linux. After reading this chapter, users should understand the use cases and limitations of Packet Tracer and be familiar with the Packet Tracer interface.

Chapter 2, Network Devices, covers Cisco network devices such as routers, switches, and other generic devices such as bridges, hubs, repeaters, and WAN emulators. Network devices enable the end devices to communicate with each other. Configuring these devices from the config tab will also be explained. By the end of this chapter, readers will be able to understand and customize network devices with modules, and save these under Custom Made Devices. Readers will also be able to configure routers and switches using the config tab without using Cisco commands.

Chapter 3, Generic IP End Devices, explains PCs, laptops, and servers at large with a brief description on other end devices such as tablets and televisions. End devices are the ones used by end users, with desktops and laptops being the most common ones.

Chapter 4, Creating a Network Topology, explains different connectors, creating network topologies, and configuring them with Cisco commands. After testing the connectivity with complex PDUs, users will also use the simulation mode to analyze the packet flow.

Chapter 5, Navigating and Modifying the Physical Workspace, introduces the physical workspace in Packet Tracer. After reading this chapter, users will understand the physical limitations of wired and wireless devices. Physical workspaces are a great way to make topologies more realistic.

Chapter 6, Configuring Routing with the CLI, guides the users to configure static and dynamic routing. A router's job is to route traffic between different networks.

Chapter 7, Border Gateway Protocol (BGP), begins with a short introduction of BGP, explains the differences between BGP and other Dynamic Routing protocols, and ends with configuring BGP in Packet Tracer. BGP is a routing protocol synonymous with ISPs.

Chapter 8, IPv6 on Packet Tracer, explains using IPv6 with Packet Tracer. IPv4 has exhausted itself and the whole world is now migrating to IPv6. By the end of this chapter, the user will be able to assign IPv6 addresses to network and end devices, configure routing between IPv6 networks, and also configure a topology with both IPv4 and IPv6.

Chapter 9, Setting Up a Wireless Network, explains the wireless devices available in Packet Tracer and makes use of the physical workspace to demonstrate the range of wireless devices. Wireless networking is being implemented everywhere.

Chapter 10, Configuring VLANs and Trunks, explains how the user will be able to create VLANs, modify trunk links between switches, configure VTP to advertise VLANs, and use simulation mode to understand broadcasts in a VLAN environment. A VLAN is used to segment a broadcast domain.

Chapter 11, Creating Packet Tracer Assessments, covers the Activity Wizard available in Packet Tracer. Wouldn't it be great to create practical questions rather than the mundane "Choose the best/correct answer" ones? By the end of this chapter, users will be able to create timed networking scenario assessments.

What you need for this book

This book is about the software called Packet Tracer that is available for download from the Cisco Networking Academy website. This software is available for both Windows and Linux operating systems.

As of the release date of this book, the latest version of Packet Tracer is Version 6. You can always find the latest version at `https://www.netacad.com/web/about-us/cisco-packet-tracer`.

Who this book is for

This book is aimed at students, instructors, and network administrators who wish to use a simulator to learn networking instead of investing in real hardware. This book assumes that the reader has a good amount of Cisco networking knowledge and will focus more on the Packet Tracer software rather than networking.

Once you've finished reading the book, you'll have a good understanding of how to use Packet Tracer to build complex topologies and also how to bring your simulations closer to reality.

Conventions

In this book, you will find a number of styles of text that distinguish between different kinds of information. Here are some examples of these styles, and an explanation of their meaning.

Any command-line input or output is written as follows:

```
chmod +x  PacketTracer601_i386_installer-rpm.bin
```

New terms and **important words** are shown in bold. Words that you see on the screen, in menus or dialog boxes for example, appear in the text like this: "Click on **Switches** from the device-type selection box and insert any switch (except **Switch-PT-Empty**) into the workspace."

Reader feedback

Feedback from our readers is always welcome. Let us know what you think about this book—what you liked or may have disliked. Reader feedback is important for us to develop titles that you really get the most out of.

To send us general feedback, simply send an e-mail to feedback@packtpub.com, and mention the book title in the subject of your message.

If there is a topic that you have expertise in and you are interested in either writing or contributing to a book, see our author guide on www.packtpub.com/authors.

Customer support

Now that you are the proud owner of a Packt book, we have a number of things to help you to get the most from your purchase.

Errata

Although we have taken every care to ensure the accuracy of our content, mistakes do happen. If you find a mistake in one of our books—maybe a mistake in the text or the code—we would be grateful if you would report this to us. By doing so, you can save other readers from frustration and help us improve subsequent versions of this book. If you find any errata, please report them by visiting http://www.packtpub.com/submit-errata, selecting your book, clicking on the **errata submission form** link, and entering the details of your errata. Once your errata are verified, your submission will be accepted and the errata will be uploaded on our website, or added to any list of existing errata, under the Errata section of that title. Any existing errata can be viewed by selecting your title from http://www.packtpub.com/support.

Piracy

Piracy of copyright material on the Internet is an ongoing problem across all media. At Packt Publishing, we take the protection of our copyright and licenses very seriously. If you come across any illegal copies of our works, in any form, on the Internet, please provide us with the location address or website name immediately so that we can pursue a remedy.

Please contact us at `copyright@packtpub.com` with a link to the suspected pirated material.

We appreciate your help in protecting our authors, and our ability to bring you valuable content.

Questions

You can contact us at `questions@packtpub.com` if you are having a problem with any aspect of the book, and we will do our best to address it.

1
Getting Started with Packet Tracer

So you have just entered the world of Cisco networking by starting to prepare for CCENT or CCNA and would like to get a taste of everything in Cisco, but do not have the luxury to afford real hardware. Well, who needs a few pieces of real hardware when you can design complex topologies with tens (if not hundreds) of Cisco devices and watch as packets move between them, and do all of this on your laptop, sitting anywhere? The best part is, if you are an instructor or interviewer, practical questions can be created with Packet Tracer; you'll learn how to do this in *Chapter 11, Creating Packet Tracer Assessments*.

This chapter will guide you through the installation of Packet Tracer, describe its graphical interface, and show you how to create your first simple topology in it. Because this is a simulator, not all real world (read real hardware) protocols are supported. So we will begin by seeing which protocols it does support.

Protocols supported by Packet Tracer

A simulator, as the name suggests, simulates network devices and its environment, so protocols in Packet Tracer are coded to work and behave in the same way as they would on real hardware. The following table shows the protocols supported by Packet Tracer:

Technology	Protocols
LAN	Ethernet (including CSMA/CD*), 802.11 a/b/g/n wireless*, and PPPOE
Switching	VLANs, 802.1q, trunking, VTP, DTP, STP*, RSTP*, multilayer switching*, EtherChannel, LACP, and PAgP
TCP/IP	HTTP, HTTPS, DHCP, DHCPv6, Telnet, SSH, TFTP, DNS, TCP*, UDP, IPv4*, IPv6*, ICMP, ICMPv6, ARP, IPv6 ND, FTP, SMTP, POP3, and VOIP(H.323)
Routing	Static, default, RIPv1, RIPv2, EIGRP, single area OSPF, multiarea OSPF, BGP, inter-VLAN routing, and redistribution
WAN	HDLC, SLARP, PPP*, and Frame Relay*
Security	IPsec, GRE, ISAKMP, NTP, AAA, RADIUS, TACACS, SNMP, SSH, Syslog, CBAC, Zone-Based Policy Firewall, and IPS
QoS	Layer 2 QoS, Layer 3 DiffServ QoS, FIFO Hardware queues, Priority Queuing, Custom Queuing, Weighted Fair Queuing, MQC, and NBAR*
Miscellaneous	ACLs (standard, extended, and named), CDP, NAT (static, dynamic, inside/outside, and overload), and NATv6

* These protocols have substantial modelling limitations, so not all commands under these protocols work.

Installing Packet Tracer

To download Packet Tracer, go to `https://www.netacad.com` and log in with your Cisco Networking Academy credentials; then, click on the Packet Tracer graphic and download the package appropriate for your operating system.

Windows

Installation in Windows is pretty simple and straightforward; the setup comes in a single file named `Packettracer_Setup6.0.1.exe`. Open this file to begin the setup wizard, accept the license agreement, choose a location, and start the installation.

Linux

Linux users with an Ubuntu/Debian distribution should download the file for
Ubuntu, and those using Fedora/Redhat/CentOS must download the file for
Fedora. Grant executable permission to this file by using `chmod`, and execute it
to begin the installation.

```
chmod +x  PacketTracer601_i386_installer-rpm.bin
./PacketTracer601_i386_installer-rpm.bin
```

Complete the installation by following on-screen instructions.

Interface overview

The layout of Packet Tracer is divided into several components similar to a photo
editor. Match the numbering in the following screenshot with the explanations
given after it:

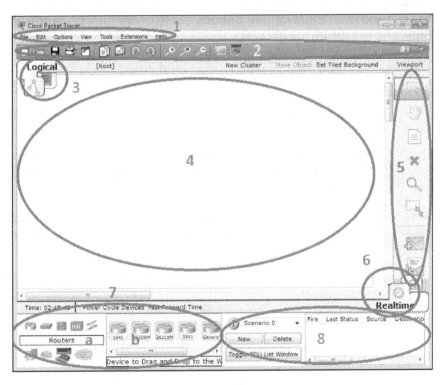

The components of the Packet Tracer interface are as follows:

- **Area 1: Menu bar** – This is a common menu found in all software applications; it is used to open, save, print, change preferences, and so on.

- **Area 2: Main toolbar** – This bar provides shortcut icons to menu options that are commonly accessed, such as open, save, zoom, undo, and redo, and on the right-hand side is an icon for entering network information for the current network.

- **Area 3: Logical/Physical workspace tabs** – These tabs allow you to toggle between the **Logical** and **Physical** work areas.

- **Area 4: Workspace** – This is the area where topologies are created and simulations are displayed.

- **Area 5: Common tools bar** – This toolbar provides controls for manipulating topologies, such as select, move layout, place note, delete, inspect, resize shape, and add simple/complex PDU.

- **Area 6: Realtime/Simulation tabs** – These tabs are used to toggle between the real and simulation modes. Buttons are also provided to control the time, and to capture the packets.

- **Area 7: Network component box** – This component contains all of the network and end devices available with Packet Tracer, and is further divided into two areas:
    - **Area 7a: Device-type selection box** – This area contains device categories
    - **Area 7b: Device-specific selection box** – When a device category is selected, this selection box displays the different device models within that category

- **Area 8: User-created packet box** – Users can create highly-customized packets to test their topology from this area, and the results are displayed as a list.

Make sure you are familiar with these names, because moving forward we will be referring to them frequently.

Creating a simple topology

Now that you're familiar with the GUI of Packet Tracer, you can create your first network topology by carrying out the following steps:

1. From the network component box, click on **End Devices** and drag-and-drop a **Generic** PC icon and a **Generic** laptop icon into the Workspace.

2. Click on **Connections**, then click on **Copper Cross-Over**, then on **PC0**, and select **FastEthernet**. After this, click on **Laptop0** and select **FastEthernet**. The link status LED should show up in green, indicating that the link is up.

3. Click on the PC, go to the **Desktop** tab, click on **IP Configuration**, and enter an IP address and subnet mask. In this topology, the default gateway and DNS server information is not needed as there are only two end devices in the network.

4. Close the window, open the laptop, and assign an IP address to it in the same way. Make sure that both of the IP addresses are in the same subnet. We'll be learning more about end device configuration in *Chapter 3, Generic IP End Devices*.

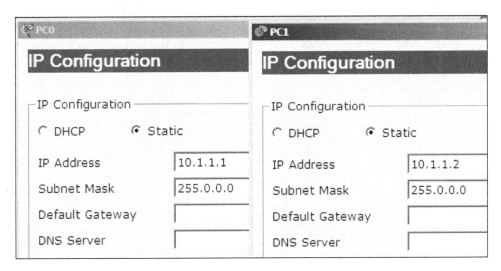

5. Close the **IP Configuration** box, open the command prompt, and ping the IP address of the device at the end to check connectivity.

```
PC>ping 10.1.1.1

Pinging 10.1.1.1 with 32 bytes of data:

Reply from 10.1.1.1: bytes=32 time=62ms TTL=128
Reply from 10.1.1.1: bytes=32 time=31ms TTL=128
Reply from 10.1.1.1: bytes=32 time=32ms TTL=128
Reply from 10.1.1.1: bytes=32 time=31ms TTL=128

Ping statistics for 10.1.1.1:
    Packets: Sent = 4, Received = 4, Lost = 0 (0% loss),
Approximate round trip times in milli-seconds:
    Minimum = 31ms, Maximum = 62ms, Average = 39ms
```

Pinging Laptop0 from PC0

What is a network topology without a single network device in it? Add an Ethernet switch to this topology so that more than two end devices can be connected, by performing the following steps:

1. Click on **Switches** from the device-type selection box and insert any switch (except **Switch-PT-Empty**) into the workspace.

2. Remove the link between the PC and the laptop using the delete tool from the common tools bar.

3. Choose the **Copper Straight-Through** cable and connect the PC and laptop with the switch. At this point, the link indicators on the switch are orange in color because the switchports are undergoing the listening and learning states of the **Spanning Tree Protocol (STP)**.

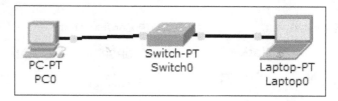

4. Once the link turns green, as shown in the previous screenshot, ping again to check the connectivity. The next chapter, *Chapter 2*, *Network Devices*, will deal with the configuration of network devices.

5. To save this topology, navigate to **File** | **Save As** and choose a location. The topology will be saved with a `.pkt` extension, with the devices in the same state.

Summary

You have successfully installed Packet Tracer and used it to create a simple topology. Keep trying different topologies with only PCs/laptops and switches to familiarize yourself with the GUI. You have also seen a list of protocols supported by Packet Tracer; use this list as a reference. Whenever you want to try a new technology in the future, make sure that the protocols to be configured are fully supported by Packet Tracer before moving ahead.

In the next chapter, you'll learn about the different types of network devices and how to customize them according to your needs. You'll also see how to configure them through the CLI as well as through the graphical interface.

2
Network Devices

Network devices form the core of networking. In this chapter, you'll learn about all of the network devices available in Packet Tracer and the modules used by it. So, after you are done customizing a device with your preferred modules, wouldn't it be nice to save them so that the device is available for use the next time? Don't know Cisco **Internetwork Operating System (IOS)** commands? After reading the *Configuring network device* section, you'll be on your feet configuring Cisco routers and switches without using any commands.

Cisco devices and Packet Tracer devices

Selecting **Switches** or **Routers** from the device-type selection box lists both Cisco devices and some devices labeled **Generic**. These are custom Packet Tracer devices running on Cisco IOS, but the slots that hold the modules are different.

Routers

A router provides connectivity between two logical networks. Every router in Packet Tracer can be switched on or off by using the provided power button.

The power switch is required to make a device simulate its real counterpart. Modules can be added or removed only after powering off the device. If the running configuration is not saved, power cycling a device will make it lose its configuration.

The following routers are available in Packet Tracer:

- **Cisco 1841**: This is an **Integrated Service Router (ISR)** having two Fast Ethernet ports, two slots for **High Speed WAN Interface Cards (HWICs)**, and one slot for **Advanced Integration Module (AIM)**

- **Cisco 1941**: This is similar to the previous model but runs on Cisco IOS Version 15. It has two ports that operate at Gigabit Ethernet speeds.

- **Cisco 2620XM**: This is a multiservice router with one Fast Ethernet port, two slots for WAN Interface cards, and one slot for AIM.

- **Cisco 2621XM**: This is similar to the previous model, except that this router has two Fast Ethernet ports.

- **Cisco 2811**: This ISR comes with two Fast Ethernet ports, four WIC slots, and a dual slot for AIM.

- **Cisco 2901**: This router has two Gigabit Ethernet ports, four WIC slots, and two **Digital Signal Processor (DSP)** slots. This router uses Cisco IOS Version 15.

- **Cisco 2911**: This router has three Gigabit Ethernet ports and all the other features of the previous router. It runs on IOS Version 15.

- **Generic Router-PT**: This is a custom router running on Cisco IOS. It contains 10 slots and has separate modules with a naming convention beginning with **PT**.

Switches

A switch, also called a multiport bridge, connects more than two end devices together. Each switch port is a collision domain. The following switches are available in Packet Tracer:

- **Cisco 2950-24**: This managed switch comes with 24 Fast Ethernet ports.

- **Cisco 2950T-24**: This switch is a member of the Catalyst 2590 Intelligent Switch family and has two Gigabit Ethernet ports in addition to the 24 Fast Ethernet ports.

- **Cisco 2960-24TT**: This is another 24 port switch; the previous switch has **Gigabit Interface Converter (GBIC)** for Gigabit Ethernet ports, whereas this switch has **Small Form-factor Pluggable (SFP)** modules for the same. Note that this is a difference only on real switches, it has no impact on Packet Tracer.

- **Cisco 3560-24PS**: This switch is different from the others because it is a layer 3 switch that can be used to perform routing in addition to switching. The **PS** suffix implies support for **Power over Ethernet (PoE)**, which can be used to power up IP phones without using power adapters.

- **Bridge PT**: This is a device used to segment a network and it has only two ports (which is why it is a bridge; if it had more, it'd be called a switch).

- **Generic Switch PT**: This is a Packet-Tracer-designed switch running on Cisco IOS. This is the only customizable switch with 10 slots and several modules.

Like the generic router, the switch section also includes a generic switch with 10 slots that can be customized with the required modules. Except for the generic switch, other Cisco model switches cannot be customized and do not have a power switch. This is because that is how real switches of the same models are designed.

Other devices

Packet Tracer has more than just Cisco routers and switches, which we'll see in this section. These devices do not have any configuration options and work out of the box.

- **Hub PT**: This network hub was the oldest way to connect multiple end devices together. It still exists in Packet Tracer so that you can simulate and learn about network storms and broadcasts. This Packet Tracer device has 10 slots.

- **Repeater PT**: This device is used to boost the signal on a wire when the distance between two points is high. We'll be using it in *Chapter 5, Navigating and Modifying the Physical Workspace*; this device has two slots.

- **Coaxial Splitter PT**: This is used to split a single coaxial connector into two. It has three coaxial ports and cannot be customized in any way.

Customizing devices with modules

A device module is a piece of hardware containing several device interfaces. For example, a **HWIC-4ESW** module contains four Ethernet (10 MBps) ports. Similar to a real router/switch, the device has to be powered off in order to add or remove modules.

The power switch is on the right-hand side of each device, with a green LED indicating that the power is on. Click on this switch to turn it off. To add a module, drag one from the modules list and drop it onto an empty slot. If a module doesn't fit into that slot, it automatically returns to the module list.

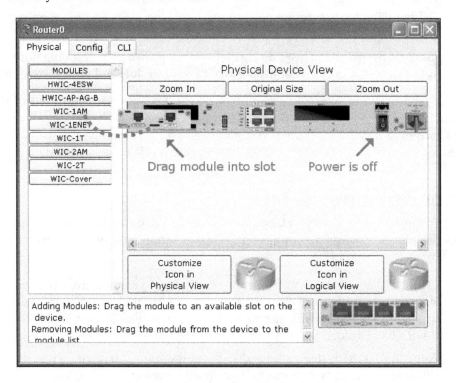

To remove a module, power off the device and drag it from the slot back to the module list.

Naming convention

Each router has more than a dozen modules but the interface they offer can be identified by their names. So, we have grouped them based on their similarities.

- **Copper Ethernet Interface**: This is the normal LAN interface, which takes in an RJ-45 connector crimped to a copper cable. Based on speeds, these interfaces are named **Ethernet** (10 MBps), **FastEthernet** (100 MBps), and **GigabitEthernet** (1000 MBps). Modules having **Ethernet** interfaces can be identified with a number followed by **E, FE, CE, CFE,** or **CGE**. Modules with **SW** provide switching features when used on routers.

    - **HWIC-4ESW** (four Ethernet switching ports)
    - **WIC-1ENET** (single Ethernet port)
    - **NM-1E** (single Ethernet port)
    - **NM-1FE-TX** (single Fast Ethernet port)
    - **NM-4E** (four Ethernet ports)
    - **NM-ESW-161** (16 Ethernet switching ports)
    - **PT-ROUTER-NM-1CE, PT-ROUTER-NM-1CFE, PT-ROUTER -NM-1CGE** (Packet Tracer custom modules)

- **Fiber Ethernet Interface**: This is similar to the previous interface, except that it uses a fiber cable. These modules are identified based on the letter **F**.

    - **NM-1FE-FX** (single Fast Ethernet fiber media)
    - **PT-ROUTER-NM-1FFE, PT-ROUTER-NM-1FGE** (Packet Tracer custom modules)

- **Serial Interface**: Modules with serial interfaces have the letter **T** or the string **A/S**. The difference is that the ones with **T** are synchronous while the **A/S** modules are asynchronous. This difference affects only production environments, but in a simulator it makes no difference.

    - **WIC-1T, WIC-2T** (a single or dual synchronous serial port)
    - **NM-4A/S, NM-8A/S** (four or eight asynchronous/synchronous serial ports)
    - **PT-ROUTER-NM-1S, PT-ROUTER-NM-1SS**

- **Modem Interface**: Modules with this interface have RJ11 ports for analog telephone cables. They are identified by having the letters **AM** present after a number as shown in the following list:
  - ° **WIC-1AM** (dual RJ11 ports for phone and modem)
  - ° **WIC-2AM, WIC-8AM** (two or eight RJ11 ports)
  - ° **PT-ROUTER-NM-1AM**

- **WICs within NMs**: Some **Network Modules** (**NM**) don't take up all the space of a slot, so they provide WIC slots within them to accommodate smaller cards. Such modules can be recognized by the letter **W** at the end of their names.

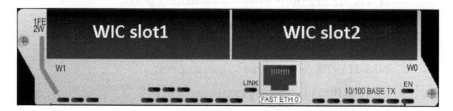

  - ° **NM-1E2W, NM-1FE2W** (a single Ethernet / Fast Ethernet port and two WIC slots)
  - ° **NM-2E2W, NM-2FE2W** (two Ethernet / Fast Ethernet ports and two WIC slots)
  - ° **NM-2W** (no interfaces, only two WIC slots)

- **Slot Covers**: Packet Tracer also provides covers for empty slots. While it makes no difference in a simulator, it can give a cleaner look when using the physical view (more information on this in *Chapter 5, Navigating and Modifying the Physical Workspace*).
  - ° **NM-Cover**: Covers a network module slot
  - ° **WIC-Cover**: Covers a WIC slot

- **HWIC-8A**: This module is new to Packet Tracer 6. It provides eight asynchronous EIA-232 connections to console ports. A router can be used as an access server if this module is plugged in.

Creating a custom device

If you require a router with a particular set of modules, it could be a daunting task to drag-and-drop modules each time before creating a topology. So Packet Tracer offers a feature to save a device that you've customized as a custom-made device. Carry out the following steps to create a custom device:

1. Drag-and-drop a network device into the work area. For this example, we'll use a **Generic** switch: **Switch-PT-Empty**.

2. Click on the switch to open its configuration dialog box, and turn the device off.

3. Add your most-used modules to this switch.

4. Navigate to **Tools | Custom Devices Dialog,** or press *Ctrl + E*.

5. Click on the **Select** button, and then click on the switch that was just customized.

6. Provide a name and description, and then click on **Add** and **Save.**

This custom device is saved with a `.ptd` extension in `%USERPROFILE%\Cisco Packet Tracer 6.0.1\templates\`; to make this custom device available to all users, copy it to `%PT5HOME%\templates\`.

Emulating WAN

To bring in more real-life scenarios, Packet Tracer has devices that emulate a WAN. Clicking on the WAN emulation cloud icon from the device-type selection box lists the following devices:

- **Cloud-PT**: This device looks like a cloud in the toolbar, but under the configuration window it looks more like a router with several slots. The following modules are available for the cloud device:

    ○ **NM-1AM**: This module provides an RJ11 connector for connecting modems using telephone cables. The interface name of this module is Modem$N$, with N being the port number.

    ○ **NM-1CE, NM-1CFE, NM-1CGE**: These three modules provide an Ethernet, Fast Ethernet, or Gigabit Ethernet interface respectively, through which the devices connected to the modem and cable interfaces can be accessed. Except for speed, all three modules perform the same function.

- ○ **NM-1FFE, NM-1FGE**: These two modules provide Fast Ethernet or Gigabit Ethernet for connecting fiber media. Functionality-wise, they perform the same function as the previous modules.

- ○ **NM-1CX**: This module has a coaxial connector for connecting a cable modem.

- ○ **NM-1S**: A serial port is available on this interface for configuring frame relay. The **Config** tab for this interface provides options for creating frame relay mappings.

- **DSL-Modem-PT**: This is a modem with an Ethernet interface and an RJ11 interface. The Ethernet interface can be switched between **Ethernet**, **FastEthernet**, and **GigibitEthernet**. This device doesn't have any configuration options.

- **Cable-Modem-PT**: This modem is similar to the previous one, except that it supports a coaxial port.

Accessing the CLI

The Command-line Interface of a device in Packet Tracer can be accessed in two ways:

- The **CLI** tab
- Console port

Although it is possible to access a device through SSH or Telnet, these are Cisco methods and are not exclusive to Packet Tracer.

The CLI tab

This is the simplest way of accessing the Command-line Interface of a device; click on a network device, navigate to the **CLI** tab, and you'll see the booting process.

The Console port

There is no difference between what is seen and controlled in this method and the previous one, but the Console Port can be used to make the topology look similar to the real world. Follow the steps to configure the console port:

1. Add a PC or a laptop to the workspace.

2. Choose connections, and then click on the console cable.

3. Connect the console cable of the network device to the RS-232 port of the PC/laptop.

4. Open the PC/laptop, navigate to the **Desktop** tab, open **Terminal**, and then with the default settings, click on **OK** to view the console. The following screenshot displays a router's console through its terminal:

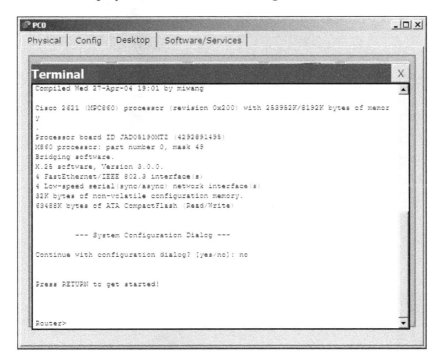

In step 2, if you use the **Automatically Choose Connection Type** option, the Ethernet ports of both of the devices will be connected.

Configuring network devices

In this section, you'll learn how to configure Cisco routers and switches without using a single command! Yes, it is possible; Packet Tracer provides a **Config** tab that contains GUI options for the most common configurations. What's more, as you tinker with the GUI, its equivalent Cisco IOS command is also displayed. Take a look at the following screenshot:

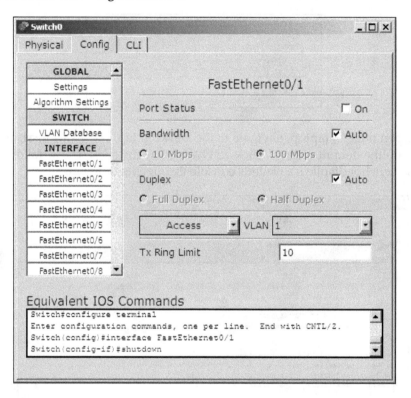

From the **Config** tab of the switch, we will set the **Interface** option to **FastEthernet0/1** and uncheck the **On** checkbox for **Port Status**. So the **Equivalent IOS Commands** section displays the following command to achieve this process:

```
Switch>enable
Switch#configure terminal
Switch(config)#interface FastEthernet0/1
Switch(config-if)#shutdown
```

Using the **Config** tab, the following can be configured:

- Global settings
- Routing (on a router and a layer 3 switch)
- VLAN database (on a switch)
- Interface settings

Let's see what options are offered under each of these sections.

Global settings

The first part of **Global settings** allows you to change the **Display name** and **Hostname** of the device. The display name can also be changed by clicking on the name below the device icon. The configuration file for the device can also be saved, erased, or exported for later use.

The **Algorithm Settings** section contains settings meant for advanced users who want to minutely tweak their device to see how it responds to certain situations. These settings can also be globally set for all network devices by navigating to **Options | Algorithm Settings,** or by using the shortcut *Ctrl + Shift + M*.

Routing

This section has options for configuring **Static** and dynamic routing (**RIP**). To configure static routing, enter the network address, netmask, and its next hop address, and then click on **Add**. Here is some sample network information:

- Network: `192.168.30.0`
- Mask: `255.255.255.0`
- Next Hop: `10.0.0.6`

To configure **Routing Information Protocol (RIP)**, it is enough to add only the network IP. Please note that the GUI uses RIP Version 1, so classless routing is not supported. Routing will be discussed in detail in *Chapter 6, Configuring Routing with the CLI*. Apart from routers, routing can also be configured on the **3560-24PS** switch, as it is a layer 3 switch.

The VLAN Database

This section will teach you how to create and remove VLANs. VLANs and trunking are discussed in *Chapter 10, Configuring VLANs and Trunks*. Only the VLAN database can be modified from these options; adding interfaces to these VLANs is what we'll see in the next section.

Interface settings

This section slightly differs from the switch and the router. Switches have options for modifying the speed and duplex setting and for assigning a port to VLAN. On routers, the VLAN section is replaced by the IP address configuration.

While changing the speed and duplex settings, if you are setting it to anything other than **auto**, make sure that the settings are the same on both ends. For example, if you set it to 100 MBps on one end and 10 MBps on the other, the link won't come up.

Summary

In this chapter, we learned a lot about network hardware devices and their modules, along with each one's features, limitations, and their naming convention. We have also seen the methods through which the CLI can be accessed. By now, you will have been able to configure these devices with just the GUI. If you are the adventurous kind, go ahead and try creating a simple topology with a couple of routers and PCs residing in different logical networks.

In the next chapter, we'll learn about the end devices available in Packet Tracer. The options in the **Config** tab of these devices will also be explored. You'll be surprised to see the number of devices available.

3
Generic IP End Devices

If network devices are the core, end devices are the ones that use this core. Packet Tracer offers a wide range of end devices, starting from PCs and laptops, to tablets, PDAs, and even a TV! In this chapter, we'll learn about each end device, the modules available for it, and its configuration options. You'll be surprised to find that these end devices support a wide array of modules; such as network devices, and also have a lot of utilities under the **Desktop** tab that match the ones you have on your real computer!

Desktops and laptops

Desktops and laptops form the highest level of configurable and usable client devices in Packet Tracer. There is no difference between them when it comes to usability; only the naming conventions of the modules are different.

The following modules are available for desktops and laptops. Similar to routers (as seen in the previous chapter), these devices too have to be switched off before adding/removing modules.

- **Linksys-WMP300N**: This provides a wireless interface for configuring WLAN on a WiFi network.

- **PC-HOST-NM-1AM**: This provides an RJ11 interface that can be used as a dial-up modem.

- **PC-HOST-NM-1CE, PC-HOST-NM-1CFE, PC-HOST-NM-1CGE**: These three modules provide an **Ethernet**, **FastEthernet**, and **GigabitEthernet** connection, respectively.

- **PC-HOST-NM-1FFE, PC-HOST-NM-1FGE**: This is the fiber Ethernet version of the previous module.
- **PC-HOST-NM-1W, PC-HOST-NM-1W-A**: Both of these modules provide a wireless interface for WLAN. The first one has a frequency of 2.4 GHz and the second 5GHz for 802.11a networks.
- **PC-HEADPHONE, PC-MICROPHONE, PC-CAMERA, PC-USB-HARD-DRIVE**: These modules serve the purpose of representing each of their respective devices. They do not have any functionality associated with them.

On laptops, the same modules are available with a different name. Instead of **HOST**, **LAPTOP** is used. So, a **PC-HOST-NM-1AM** module is named **PC-LAPTOP-NM-1AM**.

Servers

Servers are an entirely different breed when compared to other end devices. They have various functionalities and also have space for two network interfaces. The modules available for servers are the same as PC modules, except that the servers do not have the **PC-HOST-NM-1AM** module.

Looking under the **Config** tab of a server, you can see that the following services are available. Let us look at what each of these offers.

HTTP

The HTTP service offers a web server that runs both HTTP and HTTPS protocols. A textbox below the HTTP section provides options to create and edit static HTML pages. These are displayed when this server is accessed through the web browser utility of other end devices. This service is *on* by default.

DHCP

The DHCP service can be used to assign IP addresses to routers. This section has options to create and edit DHCP pools of IP addresses. It has a default pool called **serverPool**, which cannot be removed or edited. This service is *off* by default.

TFTP

The TFTP service can be immensely useful when learning about backing up and restoring Cisco IOS images and configuration files. This section lists several IOS images from routers and switches available in Packet Tracer. If any file is copied from a network device to the TFTP server, that too will be displayed. A sample is available at `Cisco Packet Tracer 6.0.1\saves\Server\TFTP\TFTP.pkt`. This service is *on* by default.

DNS

The DNS service is for resolving domain names to IP addresses. The DNS service offers the following record types: **A, CNAME, SOA**, and **NS**. Though this interface looks simple and complete, multilevel DNS setups can be configured. A sample is available at `Cisco Packet Tracer 6.0.1\saves\Server\DNS\Multilevel _DNS.pkt`.

A **DNS cache** button allows you to view cached DNS requests and has a feature that clears this cache. This service is *off* by default.

SYSLOG

This protocol provides a centralized logging service. Setting the Syslog server's IP to point to the configured server's IP from a network device fills the table in the **Config** tab with all of the logging messages generated by the device. This service is *on* by default.

AAA

AAA stands for Authentication, Authorization, and Accounting. This service is used for centrally managing the credentials of all network devices. It supports the RADIUS and TACACS authentication protocols. The options in this section allow you to create users and configure the network credentials to be used. Several samples are available at `Cisco Packet Tracer 6.0.1\saves\Server\AAA\`. This service is *off* by default.

NTP

Network Time Protocol ensures that the clocks of all devices are synchronized properly. This section has a calendar to set the date and time. Optionally, NTP authentication can also be configured. Once the server has a proper time set, all of the network devices can be configured to synchronize their clocks from this server. This service is *on* by default.

EMAIL

This section incorporates **SMTP service** and **POP3 service**. A domain name can be set and users created so that users can communicate by using the **EMAIL** option under the **Config** tab of a PC or laptop.

Only one domain is allowed per server, and either SMTP or POP3 can be switched on or off as desired.

FTP

FTP has more features as compared to **TFTP**. Users can be created and permissions can be granted to each one of them. This section also lists files that have been uploaded. There is no GUI client for accessing the **FTP** server. But the command line under the **Desktop** tab provides the FTP command-line client. A sample is available at `Cisco Packet Tracer 6.0.1\saves\Server\FTP\FTP.pkt`.

Firewall/IPv6 Firewall

Because the server has two network interfaces now, the firewall feature has been introduced in PT Version 6. This section allows you to configure inbound rules that match source/destination IP addresses and local/remote port numbers. Based on the match, the connection can either be allowed or denied.

Other end devices

Apart from PCs, laptops, and servers, Packet Tracer has a lot of end devices; some of these have no functionality while some provide interesting features.

- **Printer-PT**: This is a network printer with modules similar to a PC except for the **PC-HOST-NM-1AM** module. The only option available in this device is the IP address configuration option.

- **7960**: This is a Cisco IP phone with two Ethernet ports, one for connecting to a switch and another for connecting to a PC. The only module available is **IP_PHONE_POWER_ADAPTER**. If PoE (Power over Ethernet) is not available, this module has to be used to power the device on.

- **Home-VoIP-PT**: This device has no modules and the only configuration available is for the server address. This should be the IP address of the router on which **Communications Manager Express (CME)** has been configured. It has an Ethernet port and an RJ11 port for an analog phone.

- **Analog-Phone-PT**: This is a phone with an RJ11 connector, which, when connected to a **Home-VoIP-PT** device, can be used to make calls between Cisco IP phones.

- **TV-PT**: This television has a coaxial port and a single configuration option to turn it on or off. The screen can be viewed only in the **Physical** view of Packet Tracer. When this device is connected to **Cloud-PT**, it can be used to display a slideshow of images.

- **TabletPC-PT**: This has desktop options similar to a PC but doesn't have any modules. It has a wireless interface for connecting it to a WLAN.

- **PDA-PT**: This device is similar to the tablet we saw previously.

- **WirelessEndDevice-PT**: This is a device with a wireless interface. It has an editable GUI that uses HTML code. The **GUI** tab has Traffic Generator similar to the one available on PCs and laptops.

- **WiredEndDevice-PT**: This is similar to the previous device but has a wired interface.

Configuring end devices

End devices have a **Desktop** tab, which provides a lot of utilities for testing and debugging the network. We will learn about each utility in this section.

The following utilities are available for PCs, laptops, PDAs, and tablet PCs.

IP Configuration

We have already used the IP Configuration utility in *Chapter 1, Getting Started with Packet Tracer*, when we created a simple topology. This option is used to choose between a dynamic and static IP address. Entering a static IP address fills the **Subnet Mask** field; according to the class of the IP address, this field can also be edited if required. If **DHCP** is configured on **Server-PT**, choosing **DHCP** here obtains an IP address dynamically. Starting with Packet Tracer Version 6, this utility also has a section for configuring IPv6 addresses.

Dial-up

A modem dialer, this utility can be used if the **PC-HOST-NM-1AM** module is plugged in. This utility is available only on **PC-PT** and **Laptop-PT** devices as other end devices do not have the **NM-1AM** module. A **cloud-PT** device with phone numbers is required to be connected to this PC on one end and a router on the other end with a modem interface. A username/password combination is also required in the router; after this is done, entering them in this utility creates a connection.

Terminal

We used this utility in *Chapter 2*, *Network Devices*, for accessing the CLI through the console port. In most cases, the settings in this utility can be left to their defaults; but if you change the baud rate of the network device, it has to be changed here so that they match. This module is not available on the **Server-PT** device as it doesn't have an RS-232 interface.

Command Prompt

This utility simulates the command line offered in Windows Operating Systems. Only a limited set of commands are available but they are enough to test the network. The following are the commands available:

```
? arp delete dir ftp help ipconfig ipv6config netstat nslookup ping
snmpget snmpgetbulk snmpset ssh telnet tracert
```

Each command's supported parameters can be found by entering a command without any options as shown in the following screenshot:

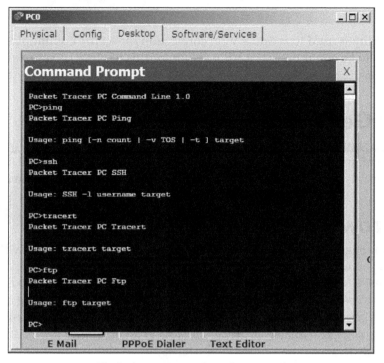

Displaying arguments for each command

Web Browser

Web Browser is a utility with minimal options, which can be used if you have a **Server-PT** device configured with HTTP. This can also be used if there is a **Linksys-WRT300N** device to access its web interface. This utility has only **back**, **forward**, **go**, and **stop** buttons and does not store any cache or history.

PC Wireless

This utility is designed for the **Linksys-WMP300N** module. It displays signal strength information and also has options for choosing a wireless network and modifying profiles to connect to wireless routers that are not broadcasting their SSID. These settings can also be saved, imported, or exported. Wireless networking will be explained in detail in *Chapter 9, Setting Up a Wireless Network*. This utility is available only on **PC-PT** and **Laptop-PT** devices, as other end devices do not have the Linksys module.

VPN

The **VPN** utility is used to create a VPN connection for secure communication. A router has to be configured as a VPN server for this to work. A sample topology is available at `Cisco Packet Tracer 6.0.1\saves\PC\VPN\Vpn_Easy.pkt`.

Traffic Generator

This utility is similar in functionality to the **Add Simple PDU** and **Add Complex PDU** tools in the common tools bar. It is used to create customized packets and send them at periodic intervals. This is immensely useful for simulating a real environment.

MIB Browser

The **MIB** (**Management Information Base**) Browser utility sends out SNMP requests. This allows you to retrieve router and switch data or make changes to the devices. A `get` request is sent to fetch a value, whereas a `set` request is sent to modify a value. A router has to be configured with an **RO** (**Read Only**) community string and **RW** (**Read Write**) community string. This utility is not available on the **Server-PT** device. A sample topology is available at `Cisco Packet Tracer 6.0.1\saves\PC\MIB_Browser\SNMP_Router.pkt`.

Cisco IP Communicator

Cisco IP Communicator is a Cisco software that can be used to turn a computer into an IP phone. This utility is available in Packet Tracer to make and answer calls using a PC or laptop. Clicking on it opens a phone GUI that can be used to dial numbers; the default TFTP server can also be changed by navigating to the **Preferences...** option, as shown in the next screenshot. This utility is not available on the **Server-PT** device.

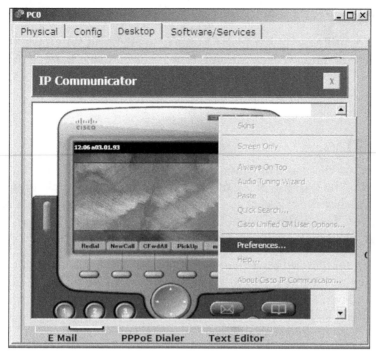

Cisco IP Communicator on the PC

E Mail

This is an e-mail client utility that can be used to send and receive e-mails. The first time it is opened, it has to be configured with the Incoming mail server (POP3), Outgoing mail server (SMTP), and credentials. A **Server-PT** device has to exist in the topology with its **EMAIL** section configured. This utility is not available on the **Server-PT** device. A sample topology is available at Cisco Packet Tracer 6.0.1\
saves\Server\Mail\mail_2Server_2PC.pkt.

PPPoE Dialer

This utility is required to establish a connection using a **DSL-Modem-PT** device. On one end, the modem device connects this PC over Ethernet and on the other end, it has a cloud connected by a phone wire. A router has to be configured as a PPPoE server with a username and password. A sample topology is available at Cisco Packet Tracer 6.0.1\saves\Router\PPPOE\client.server.modem.pppoe.pkt.

Text Editor

The **Text Editor** utility is similar to the Notepad available in Windows. It can be used to create, edit, and save text files that can be listed using the `dir` command in the command-prompt utility. Created text file can also be used to test FTP by uploading it from the command line.

Summary

In this chapter, we discussed all of the end devices available in Packet Tracer. This marks the end of the learning phase of devices. Do check the sample topologies mentioned in each section. Packet Tracer also has instructions on how to use them. Now that you are familiar with all of the devices available in Packet Tracer, their modules, and the utilities available, we will learn how to use them.

In the next chapter, we will start creating topologies that include the devices we've learnt about so far. We'll also be learning how packets move from one hop to another using the simulation mode. We will also see how to create clusters of multiple devices for a clean look.

4

Creating a Network Topology

So far, we have learned a lot about the devices available in Packet Tracer. In this chapter, we will start putting these devices to use. We'll learn what it takes to create a network topology, its connections, and link indications. Then we'll test the connectivity between the topologies and a **PDU** (**Protocol Data Unit**), both simple and complex. Once we are done with that, you'll no doubt be curious to see how data moves from one node to another. That will be taken care of by the simulation mode of Packet Tracer. Finally, we'll clean up our workspace a bit by using the clustering feature.

Connecting devices

Choosing the Connections icon from the device-type selection box lists several cables in the device-specific selection box. Packet Tracer provides the following cables that can be used to connect devices:

- **Console**: This is a console cable that is used to view the network device's console from a PC/laptop. One end of the cable connects to the console port of a network device while the other one connects to the RS-232 port on a PC/laptop.

- **Copper straight-through**: This is a standard Ethernet cable that is used to connect two devices that operate in different layers of the OSI model (such as hub to router and switch to PC). It can be used with Ethernet, Fast Ethernet and Gigabit Ethernet port types.

- **Copper cross-over**: This Ethernet cable connects devices operating in the same OSI layer (such as hub to hub, PC to PC, PC to router, and PC to printer). This cable can also be used with Ethernet, Fast Ethernet and Gigabit Ethernet port types.

- **Fiber**: This cable connects Fast Ethernet and Gigabit Ethernet ports of a fiber port.

- **Phone**: This RJ11 cable connects the analog phone to a VoIP phone or a PC's modem to a cloud. It also connects the modem interface of routers.

- **Coaxial**: The coaxial cable connects the cloud with a cable modem and a TV with the cloud.

- **Serial DCE and DTE**: Serial cables connect routers together and connect routers to the cloud. The **DCE** (**Data Circuit-terminating Equipment**) end has a clock symbol on it. Clocking must be enabled on this end using the `clock rate <300-4000000>` command to bring the line protocol up. If Serial **DTE** (**Data Terminal Equipment**) is chosen, the first device connected with this cable will be the DTE end and next device will be the DCE end. For the Serial DCE cable, this is just the opposite.

- **Octal**: This cable was introduced in PT Version 6. It has a high-density connector on one end and eight RJ45 plugs on the other.

- **Automatically choose connection type**: If you are confused about the cable to use, choosing this option automatically connects two devices with the best cable. We say best cable because if you have two routers with serial and Fast Ethernet interfaces on both of them and want to connect both of their Fast Ethernet interfaces, choosing this option will connect only their serial interfaces together. Similarly, console ports cannot be connected using this option.

Link status

After connecting devices together, you'll find a light at each end of the cable; this indicates the state of the connection, as follows:

- **Bright green**: This indicates that the physical link is up, but it doesn't indicate the status of the line protocol.

- **Blinking green**: This indicates link activity.

- **Red**: This indicates that the physical link is down. This can be caused by incorrect cables or by a port being administratively shut down.

- **Amber**: This appears only on switches, and indicates that the port is running the **STP** (**Spanning Tree Protocol**) algorithm to detect layer 2 loops.

Let us demonstrate how to connect devices in a topology containing a PC, laptop, switch, and a router. We will be using the following topology for this demo:

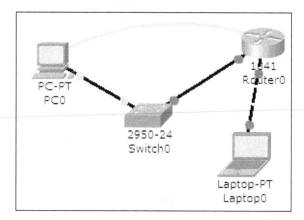

After adding the devices shown in the previous topology, click on a connection type from the device-type selection box and choose a connection. Click on a device and a context menu will list all of the interfaces available for the device. Select the interface and repeat the same steps on the other device to create a link between the two.

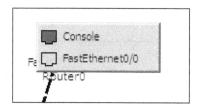

If a router is connected to any device, the link status will be red because routers have their ports in "shutdown" status by default. If a device is connected to a switch, the link is initially amber in color, indicating that it is going through the states of STP.

Testing connectivity with PDUs

Once a topology has been created, connectivity can be tested between devices by using either simple or complex PDUs. Although it is possible to do the same by pinging devices from their command-line interface, using the PDU option is quicker for large topologies.

Simple PDU

The **Add Simple PDU** option uses only **ICMP (Internet Control Message Protocol)**. We will create a topology with a PC and a server to demonstrate how this option works:

1. Add a PC and a server to the workspace and connect them using a copper crossover cable.
2. Assign IP addresses to both of them in the same subnet. Example, PC1: `192.168.0.1/255.255.255.0` and PC2: `192.168.0.2/255.255.255.0`.
3. From the common tools bar, click on the closed envelope icon or use the shortcut key *P*.
4. The pointer will change to an envelope symbol. Click on the PC first and then on the server. Now look at the **User Created Packet** box. You'll see the status as **Successful** and will also see the source, the destination, and the type of packet that was sent.

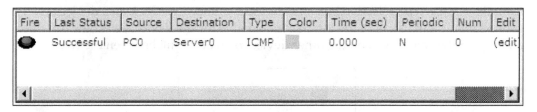

Fire	Last Status	Source	Destination	Type	Color	Time (sec)	Periodic	Num	Edit
⬤	Successful	PC0	Server0	ICMP		0.000	N	0	(edit)

That was very simple, wasn't it? Now let's see what complex PDUs have to offer.

Complex PDU

We will demonstrate complex PDUs with the same PC-Server topology:

1. Click on the open envelope icon or press *C*; this is the **Add Complex PDU** option.
2. Click on the PC and the **Create Complex PDU** dialog box opens. Select the application and fill the **Destination IP address** (IP of the server), **Starting Source Port**, and **Time** fields, and then click on the **Create PDU** button.

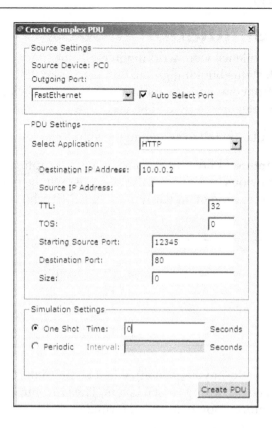

3. Now click on the server and then look at the user-created packet box. An entry indicates a successful TCP three-way handshake as shown in the following screenshot::

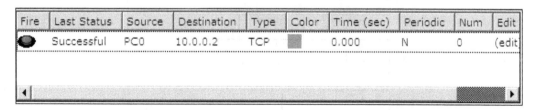

See the red button under the **Fire** column? Double clicking on it will send the same packet again.

Using the simulation mode

All of this was done while we were working in real-time mode, so the only indication of traffic was the link status blinking green. But, using simulation mode, you can see packets flowing from one node to another and can also click on a packet to see detailed information categorized by OSI layers.

Use the realtime/simulation tab to switch to the simulation mode.

Click on the **Auto Capture / Play** button to begin packet capture. Try a Simple PDU, as described in the previous section, and the event list will be populated with three entries, indicating the creation of an ICMP packet, ICMP echo sent, and ICMP reply received:

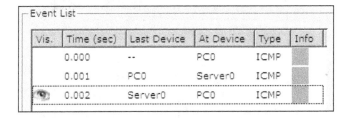

If you click on a packet (the envelope icon), you'll be presented with the packet information categorized according to OSI layers. The **Outbound PDU Details** tab lists each layer's information in a packet format:

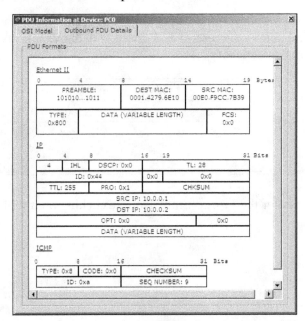

The simulation mode has a **Play Controls** section that works similar to the controls of a media player and is as follows:

- **Back**: This button moves the process one step back each time it is clicked on.

- **Auto Capture / Play**: Pressing this button results in all of the network traffic (chosen under event filters) being continuously captured until this button is pressed again.

- **Capture/Forward**: This is the manual mode of the previous button. This has to be pressed each time to move the packet from one place to another.

Clustering a topology

When large topologies are created, it becomes difficult to understand them after a while. Clustering comes to the rescue by combining several devices that you choose into a single cloud icon. Then, double-clicking on the cluster expands and displays the devices normally.

Let us see how to create a cluster:

1. We'll be using the following topology containing three switches and nine PCs. While this is not at all cluttered, it will give you an idea when to use this feature.

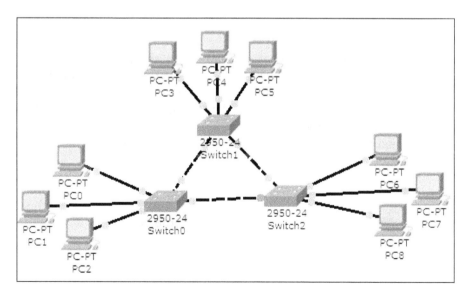

2. Click on the whitespace next to PC3; drag your mouse to select PC3, PC4, PC5, and Switch1; and click on the **New Cluster** button on the top-right corner. Repeat these steps selecting the other two sets of three PCs and a switch.

3. You'll get a clustered view as follows:

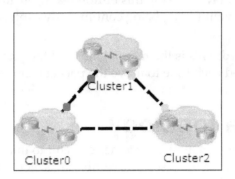

4. Double-clicking on a cluster expands it and displays only the devices within it. To go back, click on the **Back** button on the top-left corner.

Clusters can also be created inside clusters. A cluster is a feature of the logical workspace and hence does not affect how devices are displayed in the physical workspace.

Summary

In this chapter, we learned the nuances of creating a network topology in Packet Tracer, the types of connections available, and link statuses. We also saw how to test connectivity by using simple and complex PDUs. The test feature will help you a lot as you build complex topologies. Then we saw the simulation mode of Packet Tracer—go ahead and explore this mode using hubs and look at the difference between hubs and switches. Finally, we learned about creating and managing clusters.

In the next chapter, we will move the physical workspace of Packet Tracer and start creating wiring closets, offices, and entire cities! You will learn about the physical limitations of each network technology and the purpose of devices such as repeaters.

5
Navigating and Modifying the Physical Workspace

A simulator, as the name says, only logically simulates the required environment. However, Packet Tracer is much more than that. It simulates devices physically too. You've read that a copper Ethernet cable has a range of 100 meters, but have you bothered to try using it? Getting a 100 meter wire and struggling with it is not at all required as we will do just that in this chapter. Do you find the device icons boring? How about spicing things up with your own icons and background images? We will show you all this and more in this chapter.

Creating cities, offices, and wiring closets

So far, we've used the logical workspace to create topologies. The physical workspace makes your logical topology more realistic by giving it a physical dimension. The physical workspace has four environments: Intercity, City, Building, and Wiring closet.

- **Intercity**: This is the largest environment consisting of cities. Cities, buildings, and wiring closets can be created in this layer using the controls on the toolbar.

- **Cities**: This layer contains buildings and wiring closets. The default city is named **Home City**. Cities can be dragged and placed anywhere on the intercity map.

- **Buildings**: This layer contains wiring closets. The default building is named **Corporate Office**.

- **Wiring closet**: This is the final layer that contains devices placed in the logical topology. Its default name is **Main Wiring Closet** and it doesn't have any specified area.

Moving devices physically

All devices used in the logical workspace are placed in **Main Wiring Closet**; we'll learn how to move them.

1. Create a topology in the logical workspace with two PCs. Replace their default modules with **PT-HOST-NM-1FGE** (remember to switch off both the PCs before doing this) because Ethernet has distance restrictions (we'll learn more about this in the following section). Connect both of them with a fiber cable and assign IP addresses.

2. Switch to the physical view, click on the **New City** button on the yellow toolbar, and rename the newly-created city. In this example, we'll name it Remote City. Open this city and create a new building, and then create a new wiring closet within this building.

3. Use the **NAVIGATION** button and navigate to **Home City | Corporate Office | Main Wiring Closet**. This contains both the PCs we inserted in the logical workspace, as shown in the following screenshot:

4. Use the **Move Object** button (or keys *Shift + M*) and move one of the PCs to **Remote City | Office Building | Wiring Closet,** as shown in the following screenshot. This can also be done in the navigation box by using the drag-and-drop feature.

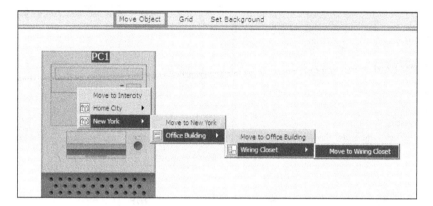

5. Navigate to the intercity and you'll find a link between home city and remote city. Now navigate to **Remote City | Office Building | Wiring Closet** to find the PC we moved.

Moving back to the logical topology, you'll see absolutely no difference in the placement of the PCs. Devices can also be moved to the intercity, cities, and buildings. In these cases, the icon of the device is displayed in the physical environment.

Managing cables and distances

The physical view adds a dimension of distance for wired and wireless devices. This is very useful for working out the placement of wireless devices.

Cable distances

Measuring a cable is as easy as placing the pointer on a cable in the physical view (as shown in the following screenshot):

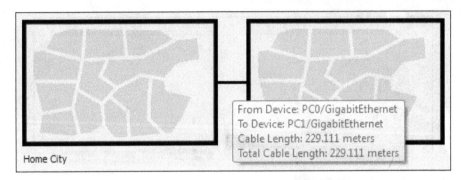

Standard copper Ethernet cables can extend up to a length of 100 meters; let's test this with the physical view:

1. Create the same two PC topologies that we used previously (as shown in the following screenshot) but use the copper cable instead of the fiber one.

2. In the physical view, move both the PCs to the intercity by following the instructions in the previous section.

3. Navigate to the intercity and check the distance between them. If the distance is less than 100 meters, move them further apart, until the distance between them is more than 100 meters.

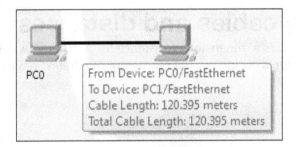

4. Now come back to the logical view and you'll find that the link status of both the PCs is red because the connection came down due to the distance.

5. Delete the link between the PCs and place a **Repeater-PT** from the hubs section. Connect both the PCs to the repeater with a copper straight-through cable. The link still remains down because this repeater was placed in the main wiring closet (which is still at a larger distance) that is very far from the intercity, as shown in the following screenshot:

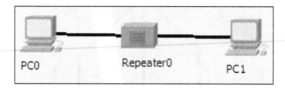

6. Move to the physical view, navigate to the **Main Wiring Closet** and move the repeater to the intercity. Go to the intercity and place the hub between the two PCs. Now you'll find that the link comes up as the repeater boosts the signal.

Cable manipulation

Let's move to the cable manipulation part of the physical workspace. Once you have a lot of devices, it becomes confusing to see which cable connects to what. Packet Tracer's physical workspace has a feature that allows cables to be color coded.

To color-code a cable, click on a wire in the physical view, choose **Color Cable** from the context menu, and pick a color from the **Select Color** dialog box. The following screenshot shows cables after they've been color coded:

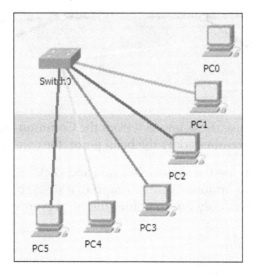

The physical workspace also has a bend point creation feature that can be used to remove the tangled look of cables. To create a bend point, click on a cable and choose **Create bendPoint** from the context menu. Any number of bend points can be created on a single link, as shown in the following screenshot:

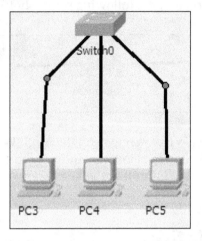

In addition, bend points can also be grouped together to form group points. To create a group point, drag a bend point and place it on another bend point. The red circle changes to a yellow square, as shown in the following screenshot:

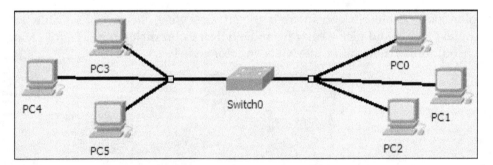

To delete a bend point, use the delete tool from the **Common Tools** bar and click on the bend point. This removes only the bend point; the connection still remains.

To delete a group point, use the same delete tool and click on the group point. A context menu contains options to either ungroup a single bend point or to ungroup all. This removes only group points; the bend points remain as it is.

Customizing icons and backgrounds

Even though Packet Tracer offers its own set of icons for each device, it is also possible to change it with our own icon. To change the icon of a device, click on it and from under the **Physical** tab click on the **Customize Icon in Logical View** button. Choose an icon from a location to change it in the logical view as shown in the following screenshot:

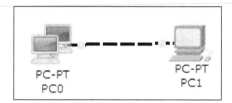

If an icon is customized in the physical view, its changes are visible only if it is placed somewhere outside the wiring closet. The backgrounds of both the logical and physical workspaces can also be customized. To change the background of the logical workspace, click on the **Set Tiled Background** button and choose an image. If the chosen image is smaller than the workspace, you can use the **Display Tiled Background Image** option.

In the physical workspace, the background can be changed for each of the intercity, city, building, and wiring closets in the same way.

Summary

In this chapter, we've learned about the physical workspace of Packet Tracer. This will help you to discover a lot of new possibilities for using wireless devices. Customizing icons and backgrounds not only improves aesthetics but also helps to differentiate between devices belonging to different organizations. In the next chapter, we will focus more on Cisco networking by explaining IP routing—both static and dynamic. The simulation mode comes very handy here, to see how things work.

Customizing icons and backgrounds

Summary

6
Configuring Routing with the CLI

We have finally reached the important part of networking—routing. Routing allows communication between multiple logical networks. When configuring routing on the command line of Packet Tracer—similar to configuring on physical hardware—you'll find that Packet Tracer offers a GUI to configure static and RIP routing protocols. In addition to this, we'll also see how load balancing works using the simulation mode, which will help you understand things better.

Static routing

Static routing is the no-brainer method for configuring routing even though it requires more work. With Packet Tracer, static routing can be configured using the GUI alone. In this method, we configure a router with a destination and a gateway to reach it. So, each router in a topology should know the means to reach all destinations in the network, which requires manual work. Similarly, if a router is added or removed from the topology, all routers must be manually updated to reflect this.

Static routing with GUI

Even if you do not know Cisco commands, this feature of Packet Tracer comes in handy. For this exercise, we will be using the topology shown in the following screenshot:.

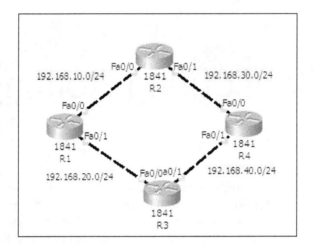

This network has four routers in a ring topology, with no PCs or loopback interfaces. Because we will be using only the GUI here, configuration will be kept to a minimum. The topology can be configured by performing the following steps:

1. Click on a router icon, go to the **Config** tab, select an interface, and configure the IP address. Make sure that you select the **On** checkbox in this section to bring the port state up. For this example, we'll be using the following IP addresses:

Router	Interface	IP Address
R1	FastEthernet0/0	192.168.10.1
	FastEthernet0/1	192.168.20.1
R2	FastEthernet0/0	192.168.10.2
	FastEthernet0/1	192.168.30.1
R3	FastEthernet0/0	192.168.20.2
	FastEthernet0/1	192.168.40.1
R4	FastEthernet0/0	192.168.30.2
	FastEthernet0/1	192.168.40.2

2. Under the **ROUTING** section, click on **Static**. The following screenshot is displayed:

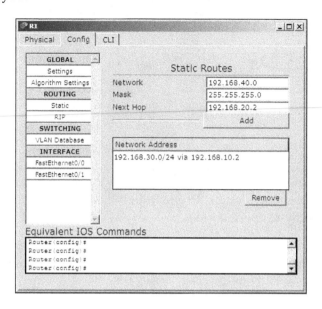

3. The following settings will be used for configuring static routing using the GUI. The concept here is to enter all routes that are not directly connected to a router and a gateway IP that belongs to a network that is directly connected.

Device	Network/Mask	Next Hop
R1	192.168.30.0 / 255.255.255.0	192.168.10.2
	192.168.40.0 / 255.255.255.0	192.168.20.2
R2	192.168.20.0 / 255.255.255.0	192.168.10.1
	192.168.40.0 / 255.255.255.0	192.168.30.2
R3	192.168.10.0 / 255.255.255.0	192.168.20.1
	192.168.30.0 / 255.255.255.0	192.168.40.2
R4	192.168.10.0 / 255.255.255.0	192.168.30.1
	192.168.20.0 / 255.255.255.0	192.168.40.1

4. Now use simple PDU and test the connectivity between all of the routers. Then use the simulation mode to find the route taken by the packets.

5. How about taking a look at the routing table? For this, too, the GUI has an option; click on the inspect icon or press *I* and select a router. A table containing four routes will appear for each router, as shown in the following screenshot:

Routing Table for R1				
Type	Network	Port	Next Hop IP	Metric
C	192.168.10.0/24	FastEthernet0/0	---	0/0
C	192.168.20.0/24	FastEthernet0/1	---	0/0
S	192.168.30.0/24	---	192.168.10.2	1/0
S	192.168.40.0/24	---	192.168.20.2	1/0

But we configured only two routes, so why four? The extra two routes are the subnets of the directly-connected links.

In this topology, even though there is an alternate route to each network, only one route is used because this is how we have configured it. We'll learn more about having more than one route in the *Load Sharing* section.

Static routing with the CLI

The configuration and the topology will be same in this section. We'll only see the commands required for one device. The topology can be configured by performing the following steps:

1. Assign IP addresses to the interfaces on each router using the following commands:

```
R1(config)#interface FastEthernet0/0
R1(config-if)#ip address 192.168.10.1 255.255.255.0
R1(config-if)#no shutdown
R1(config-if)#exit
R1(config)#interface FastEthernet0/1
R1(config-if)#ip address 192.168.20.1 255.255.255.0
R1(config-if)#no shutdown
R1(config-if)#exit
```

2. Configure static routing with the `ip route` command, using the following syntax:

    ```
    R1(config)#ip route <Destination Prefix> <Destination prefix mask>
    <Gateway IP>
    ```

3. For router **R1**, the following commands are used:

    ```
    R1(config)#ip route 192.168.30.0 255.255.255.0 192.168.10.2

    R1(config)#ip route 192.168.40.0 255.255.255.0 192.168.20.2
    ```

Use simple PDU to test the connectivity. If you get message indicating a failure, switch to simulation mode and see which router is incorrectly configured.

Dynamic routing protocols

When we learned about static routing we found that a lot of manual configuration was involved and a change to the topology also required manual configuration changes. Dynamic protocols work by advertising routes to each other.

The configuration is the opposite of static routing; here, we enable dynamic routing on the required interfaces. The routing protocol then forms "neighborship" with other routers and sends them the directly-connected routes and other received routes. In this way, all routers exchange updates with one another. When a topology change occurs, those updates are also sent out by routers that learn about this loss of connectivity.

Configuring RIP with the GUI

Packet Tracer offers a GUI to configure a dynamic routing protocol called **RIP (Routing Information Protocol)**. This GUI section is similar to the static routing section. It has only one textbox for entering the network address of the directly connected network.

You may think that the rest of the configuration is similar to the **Static** configuration, but it isn't. Whereas in the static configuration we entered routes of other routers, in RIP, we enter the network IP addresses of the router's interfaces. By doing this, you are enabling that routing protocol on a particular interface. To configure dynamic routing with the GUI, perform the following steps:

4. Create the same four-router topology we used previously and assign the same IP addresses through the **Config** tab.

5. Click on **RIP**—now, configuring this is very easy, with each router requiring only the **Network** IP of its own interfaces, as shown in the following screenshot:

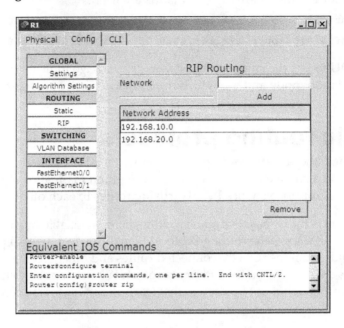

6. Enter the following network IP addresses:

Device	RIP Network
R1	192.168.10.0
	192.168.20.0
R2	192.168.10.0
	192.168.30.0
R3	192.168.20.0
	192.168.40.0
R4	192.168.30.0
	192.168.40.0

7. Once the topology is configured, use the simple PDU to check for connectivity. Let's check for two indirectly connected routers (**R1** and **R4** or **R2** and **R3**). Once the connection is successful, let's see how dynamic routing works on topology changes.

8. Use the delete tool and remove either the link between **R1** and **R2** or the link between **R1** and **R3**. Use the simulation mode and test connectivity with the simple PDU. You'll find that the packet takes the alternate, longer route and succeeds in reaching the destination.

If you have tried step 5 of the static routing topology, the packet would've failed as we did not enter any alternate gateway to each destination network. This is the biggest advantage of using a dynamic routing protocol.

Configuring RIP with the CLI

Let's do the same thing using the CLI tab. The commands are very simple and if you have noticed the **Equivalent IOS Commands** section under the **Config** tab, you'll know them already. To configure dynamic routing by using the **CLI** tab, perform the following steps:

1. Use the same commands used in the **Static** section to assign IP addresses to the interfaces.

2. Then, from the global configuration mode, enter into the config mode of RIP by issuing the following command:

   ```
   R1(config)#router rip
   ```

3. Use the `network` command, followed by the network IP address. For the device **R1**, use the following commands:

   ```
   R1(config-router)#network 192.168.10.0
   R1(config-router)#network 192.168.20.0
   ```

4. Configure all the other routers in the same way. Use the simple PDU to test the connectivity.

Now that you know how to configure basic static and dynamic routing, let's move to the routing table.

The Routing table

A routing table lists all of the preferred routes known to a router. It is viewable in two ways, one using the inspect tool of packet tracer and the other using the `show ip route` Cisco IOS command. With each way, you'll see a table with lots of columns and information. We are about to see what each of these means. Here is a sample output of a command used to show the routing table:

```
R1>show ip route

C    192.168.10.0/24 is directly connected, FastEthernet0/0

R    192.168.20.0/24 [120/1] via 192.168.10.1, 00:00:18,
FastEthernet0/0

C    192.168.30.0/24 is directly connected, FastEthernet0/1

R    192.168.40.0/24 [120/1] via 192.168.30.2, 00:00:08,
FastEthernet0/1
```

The first column denotes the routing protocol. The letter `C` is for connected and `R` is for RIP; if you check the routing table after configuring static routing, you'll find the letter `S`.

The next column is the destination network. After this, comes the **administrative distance (AD)** – the first number inside the square brackets; this specifies which routing protocol takes priority. The second number in the square brackets, after the slash, is the **metric** of this route. On RIP, the number of hops to reach a destination is used as the metric. RIP has an AD of `120` and static routing has `1`.

So, if a router has two routes for the same destination network via both static routing and RIP, static routing will be used as it has a lower AD.

The IP address after `via` is the gateway's IP, also know as the **next hop IP** through which this route is reached. The time clock after that is called the **Holddown timer**. In any dynamic routing protocol, messages are sent at a certain interval (30 seconds in RIP). Each time a **hello** message is received, this timer is reset. If no response is received within 180 seconds this route is removed or an alternate route is found.

The final column is the outgoing interface to reach the gateway.

Load sharing

In the topology we have being configuring throughout this chapter, we can find that each router has two paths to reach each destination. So how about seeing how routers use these multiple paths together and load balancing the traffic across them.

Load balancing with RIP

We take RIP first because we do not have to do anything specific for load balancing. If there are multiple paths to reach a network destination with the same metric, RIP automatically load balances them. We will be using an interface type known as **loopback** to achieve this. A loopback is a virtual interface that behaves like a real interface and takes IP addresses.

We'll use the same topology we've been using throughout this chapter, and just add an extra interface. On router **R4**, we will add a loopback interface by using the following steps:

1. Unfortunately, it isn't possible to do this with the GUI, so go to the **CLI** tab of **R4** and enter the following commands:

   ```
   R4(config)#interface loopback 0
   R4(config-if)#ip address 192.168.100.0 255.255.255.0
   ```

2. Now on the same router, let's enable this interface for RIP. Go to the RIP config mode and enter the network IP of this interface.

   ```
   R4(config)#router rip
   R4(router-if)#network 192.168.100.0
   ```

3. That's it, create a complex PDU that is sent every two seconds.

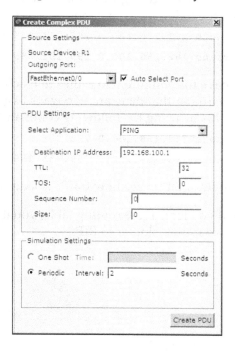

4. Switch over to the simulation mode and you'll find that the first packet takes the **R1-R2-R4** route while the second takes the **R1-R3-R4** route.

You can also see which routes are load balanced by looking into the following routing table:

```
Router>show ip route
R     192.168.30.0/24 [120/1] via 192.168.10.2, 00:00:12, FastEthernet0/0
R     192.168.40.0/24 [120/1] via 192.168.20.2, 00:00:14, FastEthernet0/1
R     192.168.100.0/24 [120/2] via 192.168.20.2, 00:00:08, FastEthernet0/1
                       [120/2] via 192.168.10.2, 00:00:08, FastEthernet0/0
```

Only the RIP routes are shown here. Note that the route `192.168.100.0/24` has two gateways; this indicates that traffic to this network is load balanced.

Load balancing with static routing

Static routing requires additional configuration for a route to be load balanced. Assign IP addresses to all physical interfaces and also configure loopback interfaces as explained in the RIP section. To configure a load balanced route with static routing, perform the following steps:

1. Go to router **R2** and **R3** and configure a route to the **R4** router's loopback interface by using the following commands:

   ```
   R2(config)#ip route 192.168.100.0 255.255.255.0 192.168.30.2
   R3(config)#ip route 192.168.100.0 255.255.255.0 192.168.40.2
   ```

2. Now for **R1**, we have to configure two routes to reach `192.168.100.0/24`. We need to tell the router that there are two ways to get to the **R4** router's loopback. We do this by using the following commands:

   ```
   R1(config)#ip route 192.168.100.0 255.255.255.0 192.168.10.2
   R1(config)#ip route 192.168.100.0 255.255.255.0 192.168.20.2
   ```

3. Use the same complex PDU to see how traffic is load balanced.

After this configuration, if you look at the routing table, you'll find the network `192.168.100.0/24` has two routes, similar to RIP.

Summary

In this chapter, we saw how to configure static and dynamic routing with RIP in Cisco Packet Tracer. By now you will understand the differences between both of them and
the pros and cons of each of them. We also saw configuring load balancing with both RIP and static routing.

In the next chapter, we will talk only about a single routing protocol called **Border Gateway Protocol** (**BGP**). Although it is also a dynamic routing protocol, it differs to a great extent from other dynamic routing protocols.

7
Border Gateway Protocol (BGP)

The Internet is a huge network and is made up of many smaller networks. To learn about routes in other networks, each network has to run a routing protocol. While protocols such as **EIGRP (Enhanced Interior Gateway Routing Protocol)**, **OSPF (Open Shortest Path First)**, and **RIP (Routing Information Protocol)** work well for many networks, they do not scale to support the needs of a gigantic network like the Internet, nor do they provide the level of administrative separation required. So, **BGP (Border Gateway Protocol)** is used by **ISP (Internet Service Provider)** and large enterprises to advertise IP routes to one another.

In this chapter, we'll learn about BGP and its features when compared to other routing protocols. We will also learn the commands used in BGP and configure it in Cisco Packet Tracer.

What is BGP?

BGP is a very robust routing protocol that is used to exchange routing information between multiple **Autonomous Systems (AS)**. This brings up the question of what an AS is. An AS is a collection of IP prefixes (read IP networks) that are maintained by a network operator. This network operator could be an enterprise or an ISP.

Each AS has a number assigned to it called **ASN (Autonomous System Number)**. Public AS numbers are assigned by the **IANA (Internet Assigned Numbers Authority)** to the **RIRs (Regional Internet Registries)**. These RIRs, in turn, assign them to individual enterprises or ISPs.

Configuration of BGP largely depends on how an organization is connected to an ISP. There are four possible ways in which this can be done:

- **Single homed (one link to one ISP)**: This is the simplest design (shown in the following screenshot) and has one link from the enterprise connecting to the ISP. This design has no redundancy or failover:

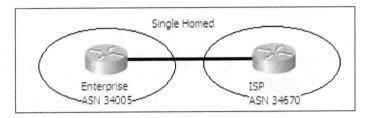

- **Dual homed (two or more links to one ISP)**: This design has a single ISP but has two or more links connecting to it. This provides some amount of reliability in the event of link issues. The following screenshot has examples of dual homed design:

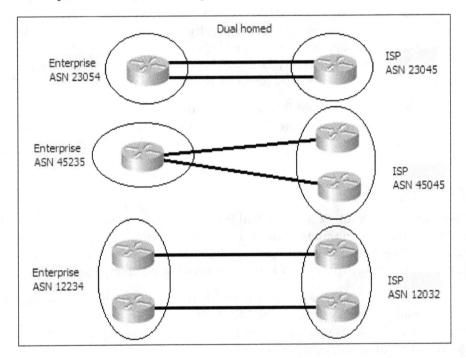

- **Single multihomed (one link to two or more ISPs)**: This case (shown in the following screenshot) has multiple ISPs with one link connecting to each of them:

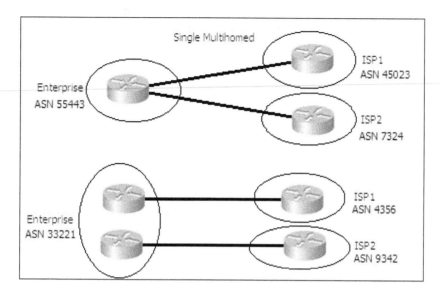

- **Dual mutihomed (two or more links per ISP to two or more ISPs)**: This design (shown in the following screenshot) provides the highest level of reliability and availability. In this case, there are two or more ISPs with two or more links connecting each of them:

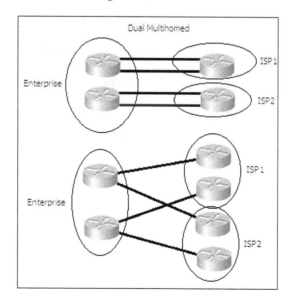

BGP may not always be used in all the previously-discussed designs. For some designs such as single homed, it is better to just have a static default route in the enterprise router towards the ISP, and another on the ISP side for just the network prefix of the enterprise. However, implementing BGP on multihomed networks ensures that the most efficient route is used as these networks have two or more links to ISP(s).

There are two types of BGP:

- eBGP (External BGP)
- iBGP (Internal BGP)

External BGP

This type of BGP is used to exchange routes between two types of AS. The administrative distance of eBGP is 20. By default, the update packets in eBGP have the TTL set to 1, so that only directly connected BGP routers receive it. However, this behavior can be changed by using commands. Also, an eBGP peer will advertise all the valid routes it has learned from its eBGP and iBGP peers. When an eBGP neighbor advertises a route, it sets the next-hop field of the route to its own address.

Internal BGP

This type of BGP is used to exchange routes within an AS. The administrative distance of iBGP is 200. Updates in iBGP do not have TTL value limitations. An iBGP peer does not advertise a route to another iBGP peer if the route was learned via iBGP. This is done to prevent routing loops within an AS. The next-hop field of the route updates remains unchanged when one iBGP peer advertises to another iBGP peer. This behavior can be modified with the use of commands.

[Cisco Packet Tracer Version 5.3.3 does *not* support iBGP.]

BGP versus dynamic routing protocols

Even though BGP works like any other routing protocol, it differs from them a lot. **IGPs (Interior Gateway Protocols)** such as RIP, OSPF, and EIGRP are enabled interface-wise. The network statement in the routing protocol configuration is used to mention a network IP address, and all interfaces' IP addresses that fall within the specific network range have a particular protocol enabled. On these enabled interfaces, these IGPs send out broadcast or multicast messages containing network route information. For this to work, two routers running IGPs have to be directly connected. The metrics used by IGPs to choose the best path are the number of hops, bandwidth, delay, and so on.

On the other hand, BGP doesn't have the concept of interfaces because the entire router is considered to be in the AS. Its neighbors are not automatically discovered and have to be mentioned statically with the `neighbor` command. After this, BGP messages are unicasted to TCP packets. BGP runs on TCP port 179 and listens to BGP messages. A neighbor doesn't have to be directly connected and can be several hops away. But, by default, the TTL value of a BGP message is 1. So, if a peer is not directly connected, it has to be increased. BGP's way of choosing the best path is entirely different from IGPs. It uses a variety of **path attributes (PA)** such as `next hop reachability`, `weight`, and `AS_PATH` (number of ASs in the path to the destination). Moreover, BGP is designed for handling hundreds of thousands of IP routes, which consumes a lot of resources if done with an IGP.

Configuring BGP in Packet Tracer

First, let's look at the commands used in BGP:

```
router bgp <asn>
```

For example:

```
R1(config)#router bgp 120
```

This command enables BGP on a router and moves to the router configuration mode. The ASN can be any value between 1 and 65535. Once enabled, the BGP process must choose a router ID. By default, BGP uses the following methods priority-wise, to pick a router ID.

- **Configured**: This is the router ID configured by using the `bgp router-id` router subcommand
- **Highest loopback**: This is the highest numeric IP address configured on any up loopback interface at the time the BGP process is initialized
- **Highest other interfaces**: This is the highest numeric IP address configured on any up non-loopback interface at the time the BGP process is initialized

A router ID can be explicitly configured using the following command:

```
bgp router-id X.X.X.X
```

For example, we can use the following command to configure the router ID:

```
R1(config-router)#bgp router-id 1.1.1.1
```

For configuring a BGP neighbor, we can use the following command:

```
R1(config-router)#neighbor X.X.X.X remote-as <asn>
```

For example:

```
R1(config-router)#neighbor 10.0.0.2 remote-as 130
```

The ASN entered for `remote-as` should be the ASN of the neighboring router. This changes in eBGP and is the same in iBGP. Let us look at an example.

The following commands are used to change the eBGP:

```
R1(config)#router bgp 120
R1(config-router)#neighbor 10.0.0.2 remote-as 130
```

The following commands are used to change the iBGP:

```
R1(config)#router bgp 120
R1(config-router)#neighbor 192.168.1.20 remote-as 120
```

As mentioned earlier, when exchanging routes within an AS, iBGP doesn't modify the next-hop field. This can become problematic because the next hop is the IP of the neighboring AS's router, and unless it is redistributed by using an IGP, the internal network will reject the routes because the next hop is invalid. So, the following command sets its own IP as the next-hop of a route:

```
R1(config-router)#neighbor X.X.X.X next-hop-self
```

BGP also has a network command. This is used to specify a route that will be advertised in BGP. This route should exist in the routing table to be advertised in BGP:

```
R1(config-router)#network 10.20.20.0 mask 255.255.255.0
```

It is also possible to omit the mask command, doing which it takes the network as a classful one.

There are a lot of other commands in BGP that Packet Tracer doesn't support, so we'll go ahead and configure a topology using these commands.

For this exercise, we'll use a single mutihomed design (shown in the following screenshot) as Packet Tracer doesn't support iBGP:

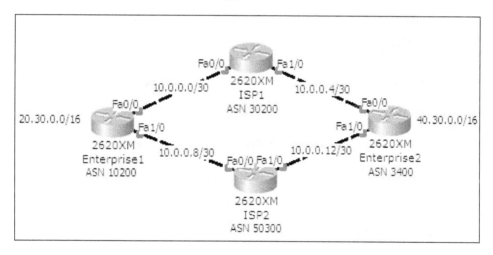

This topology has four routers—two belonging to different enterprises and the other two belonging to different ISPs. Both the enterprise routers have loopback interfaces configured with the IP addresses shown in the topology. This is to demonstrate the injecting of routes into BGP.

The following table lists the interfaces and their IP addresses:

Device	Interface	IP address / Subnet Mask
Enterprise1	Loopback0	20.30.0.1 / 255.255.0.0
	FastEthernet0/0	10.0.0.1 / 255.255.255.252
	FastEthernet1/0	10.0.0.9 / 255.255.255.252
Enterprise2	Loopback0	40.30.0.1 / 255.255.0.0
	FastEthernet0/0	10.0.0.5 / 255.255.255.252
	FastEthernet1/0	10.0.0.13 / 255.255.255.252
ISP1	FastEthernet0/0	10.0.0.2 / 255.255.255.252
	FastEthernet1/0	10.0.0.6 / 255.255.255.252
ISP2	FastEthernet0/0	10.0.0.10 / 255.255.255.252
	FastEthernet1/0	10.0.0.14 / 255.255.255.252

The following are the steps to configure BGP on the meshed network topology:

1. Let's start configuring BGP on the enterprise routers:

```
Enterprise1(config)#router bgp 10200
Enterprise1(config-router)# bgp router-id 0.0.0.1
Enterprise1(config-router)#neighbor 10.0.0.2 remote-as 30200
Enterprise1(config-router)# neighbor 10.0.0.10 remote-as 50300
Enterprise1(config-router)# network 20.30.0.0 mask 255.255.0.0


Enterprise2(config)#router bgp 3400
Enterprise2(config-router)# bgp router-id 0.0.0.2
Enterprise2(config-router)#neighbor 10.0.0.6 remote-as 30200
Enterprise2(config-router)# neighbor 10.0.0.14 remote-as 50300
Enterprise2(config-router)# network 40.30.0.0 mask 255.255.0.0
```

2. Now let's configure the ISP routers:

```
ISP1(config)#router bgp 30200
ISP1(config-router)# bgp router-id 1.1.1.1
ISP1(config-router)# neighbor 10.0.0.1 remote-as 10200
ISP1(config-router)# neighbor 10.0.0.5 remote-as 3400
```

```
ISP2(config)#router bgp 50300
ISP2(config-router)# bgp router-id 2.2.2.2
ISP2(config-router)#neighbor 10.0.0.9 remote-as 10200
ISP2(config-router)# neighbor 10.0.0.13 remote-as 3400
```

3. You should now see console messages indicating that a BGP neighbor is up:

```
%BGP-5-ADJCHANGE: neighbor 10.0.0.9 Up
%BGP-5-ADJCHANGE: neighbor 10.0.0.13 Up
```

4. Now try pinging from **Enterprise1** to the loopback address of **Enterprise2**:

```
Enterprise1>ping 40.30.0.1


Type escape sequence to abort.
Sending 5, 100-byte ICMP Echos to 40.30.0.1, timeout is 2
seconds:
Success rate is 0 percent (0/5)
```

5. We see that it fails. This is because the ICMP request packet uses a source address of `10.0.0.1`, so when this packet is received by **Enterprise2**, it doesn't have a route to `10.0.0.0/30` for sending a reply. We used the network command to inject only the routes of loopback addresses, hence we shall use the source address of the loopback itself using an extended ping:

```
Enterprise1>enable
Enterprise1#ping
Protocol [ip]:
Target IP address: 40.30.0.1
Extended commands [n]: y
Source address or interface: loopback0
Type escape sequence to abort.
Sending 5, 100-byte ICMP Echos to 40.30.0.1, timeout is 2
seconds:
Packet sent with a source address of 20.30.0.1
!!!!!
Success rate is 100 percent (5/5), round-trip min/avg/max =
62/62/63 ms
```

6. So, we have successfully configured eBGP. Let us take a look at the routing table of BGP:

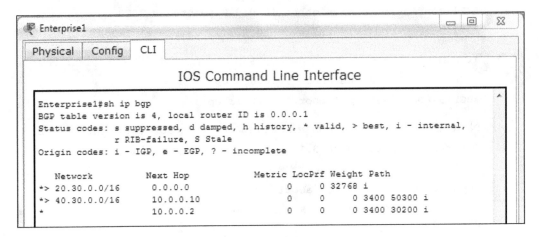

If you look at the **Path** column, you can see the ASNs that come in the path to the destination. The > symbol indicates a preferred route.

Summary

In this chapter, we learned the various designs used by organizations to connect to the Internet. Then we saw the widely used routing protocol BGP, its features when compared to IGPs, and its configuration. Sadly, Packet Tracer doesn't support iBGP, but if you can get your hands on the real hardware or **dynamips**, do try it out.

In the next chapter, we will learn about the latest game changer of networks—IPv6. We will start by learning how to assign IP addresses to it and then go about configuring routing. Finally, we'll learn how to use both IPv4 and IPv6 in a network.

8

IPv6 on Packet Tracer

IPv4 has 4.3 billion addresses, which may seem mindboggling. However, it took only two decades for it to reach its depletion. IPv6 has come to the rescue in the form of 128-bit addresses. Packet Tracer supports a wide array of IPv6 features. We'll start by learning how to assign IP addresses to different devices and how to configure routing between them. Finally, we'll create a setup that enables IPv6 communication over IPv4 devices.

Assigning IPv6 addresses

Starting from Packet Trace Version 6, the **IP Configuration** utility under the **Desktop** tab of end devices has an option to enter an IPv6 address. Let's begin with a simple topology consisting of two PCs and a router connected to a switch, as shown in the following screenshot:

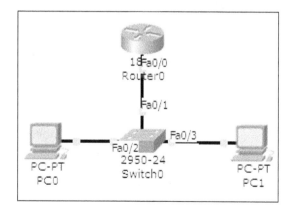

There are three ways of assigning IPv6 addresses to a device and we'll see each one of them.

Autoconfiguration

Autoconfiguration requires the least amount of configuration but makes it difficult to remember the IPv6 addresses. This method uses the MAC address of the device to create an IPv6 address with the FE80:: prefix. Carry out the following steps to assign IPv6 addresses using Autoconfiguration:

1. Begin by configuring the router. Enter the interface configuration mode and enable IPv6 on the interface.

   ```
   R0(config)#ipv6 unicast-routing
   R0(config)#interface FastEthernet0/0
   R0(config-if)#ipv6 enable
   ```

2. Next, we will configure a link local address and a global unicast address on this interface. We'll use eui-64 to reduce the configuration.

   ```
   R0(config-if)#ipv6 address autoconfig
   R0(config-if)#ipv6 add 2000::/64 eui-64
   R0(config-if)#no shutdown
   ```

3. Verify that the interface is up and has two IPv6 addresses.

   ```
   R0>sh ipv6 interface brief
   FastEthernet0/0                [up/up]
       FE80::2D0:58FF:FE65:E701
       2000::2D0:58FF:FE65:E701
   ```

4. These IPv6 addresses may vary when you try them out, as they are based on the MAC address. Enable routing so that this router can be identified as a default gateway.

   ```
   R0(config)#ipv6 unicast-routing
   ```

5. The configuration of the router is now done, let's move on to the PCs. Go to the **Desktop** tab of the PC, open **IP Configuration**, and under the **IPv6 Configuration** section, choose **Auto Config**. The gateway and the PC's IP address will be assigned automatically, as shown in the following screenshot:

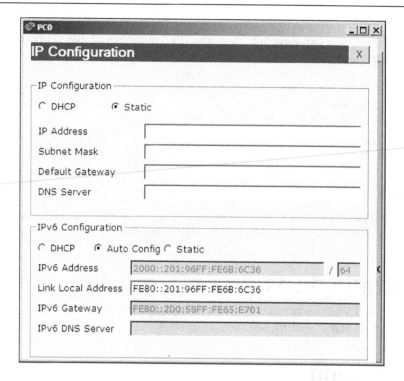

6. Use the simple PDU tool to test the connectivity; you'll see ICMPv6 packets moving between the nodes. To view the IPv6 address from the command line of PCs, use the `ipv6config` command.

Static IPv6

IPv6 addresses can also be assigned statically on all devices. We'll use the same topology for this section too. We'll carry out the following steps to configure IPv6 addresses statically:

1. Begin by configuring a static IPv6 address on the router.

    ```
    R0(config)#interface fastethernet0/0
    R0(config-if)#ipv6 enable
    R0(config-if)#ipv6 address 2000::1/64
    R0(config-if)#no shutdown
    ```

2. Go to the **Desktop** tab of PC, open the **IP Configuration** utility, and enter an IPv6 address with the same prefix.

3. Now use the simple PDU tool to test the connectivity. Once both the methods work fine, you can have a look at the IPv6 neighbors table. This is similar to the ARP table of IPv4.

```
R0#sh ipv6 neighbor
IPv6 Address                                    Age Link-layer Addr
State Interface
2000::2                                           0 00E0.A39E.05C4
REACH Fa0/0
2000::3                                           0 0001.43B9.0268
REACH Fa0/0
```

Now that we have configured IPv6 addresses on a single network, let's configure them on more networks and enable routing between them.

IPv6 static and dynamic routing

Similar to IPv4, IPv6 too supports both static and dynamic routing. Configuration commands for its static routing are similar to IPv4.

Static routing

Modifying the same topology that we used previously, let's add a router, switch, and two PCs to create a separate network, as shown in the following screenshot:

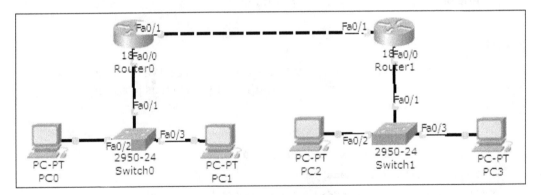

The first network will use addresses starting from `2000:1::/64` and the second network will use addresses starting from `2000:2::/64`. The link between both the routers will have IP addresses `2001::10/64` and `2001::20/64`.

Here is a table describing the topology:

Device	Interface	IP address
R1	FastEthernet0/0	2000:1::1/64
	FastEthernet0/1	2001::10/64
PC0	FastEthernet	2000:1::2/64
PC1	FastEthernet	2000:1::3/64
R2	FastEthernet0/0	2000:2::1/64
	FastEthernet0/1	2001::20/64
PC2	FastEthernet	2000:2::2/64
PC3	FastEthernet	2000:2::3/64

After the necessary IP addresses and gateways have been assigned, open the **CLI** tab for the **R1** router, and start configuring routing by following the given commands:

```
R1(config)#ipv6 unicast-routing
R1(config)#ipv6 route 2000:2::/64 2001::20
```

Next, open the **CLI** tab for **R2** and configure routing on it.

```
R2(config)#ipv6 unicast-routing
R2(config)#ipv6 route 2000:1::/64 2001::10
```

Now use the simple PDU tool to test the connectivity. You may also use the `tracert` command on a PC to see the path a packet takes.

```
PC>tracert 2000:2::3


Tracing route to 2000:2::3 over a maximum of 30 hops:

  1    63 ms      63 ms      47 ms      2000:1::1
  2    94 ms      78 ms      94 ms      2001::20
  3    156 ms     109 ms     129 ms     2000:2::3


Trace complete.
```

Dynamic routing

Packet Tracer offers the same dynamic routing protocols for IPv6: RIPv6, EIGRP, and OSPF. We'll be configuring RIPv6 in this section. Note that RIPv6 does not represent RIP Version 6; it is RIP for IPv6 addresses.

For this exercise, we'll use the topology shown in the following screenshot:

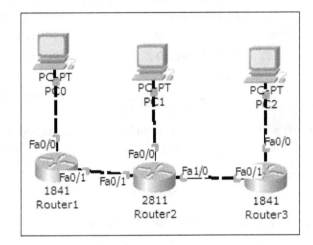

The additional IP assignment details alone are shown in the following table:

Device	Interface	IPv6 Address
R2	FastEthernet1/0	2001:1::10/64
R3	FastEthernet0/0	2000:3::1/64
	FastEthernet0/1	2001:1::20/64
PC2	FastEthernet	2000:3::2/64

We'll see how to configure RIP on one router and you can do the same on the others.

```
R1(config)#interface FastEthernet0/0
R1(config-if)#ipv6 address 2000:1::1/64
R1(config-if)#ipv6 rip Net1 enable
R1(config-if)#ipv6 enable
R1(config-if)#interface FastEthernet0/1
R1(config-if)#ipv6 address 2001::10/64
R1(config-if)#ipv6 rip Net1 enable
R1(config-if)#ipv6 enable
```

Note that the `ipv6 rip` command is used to enable RIP on a particular interface. Entering `ipv6 rip Net1 enable` on the first interface begins the RIPv6 process. The `Net1` string can be any name that can be used to name the RIP process. Once configured, use the usual diagnostic tools (ping to simple PDU) to check the connectivity. To view the RIP database, use the following command:

```
R1#sh ipv6 rip database
RIP process "Net1" local RIB
 2000:2::/64, metric 2, installed
    FastEthernet0/1/FE80::201:97FF:FE87:E5A9, expires in 173 sec
 2000:3::/64, metric 3, installed
    FastEthernet0/1/FE80::201:97FF:FE87:E5A9, expires in 173 sec
 2001::/64, metric 2
    FastEthernet0/1/FE80::201:97FF:FE87:E5A9, expires in 173 sec
 2001:1::/64, metric 2, installed
    FastEthernet0/1/FE80::201:97FF:FE87:E5A9, expires in 173 sec
RIP process "LINK" local RIB
```

Trace the route of the packet to see the path it takes.

```
PC>tracert 2000:3::2


Tracing route to 2000:3::2 over a maximum of 30 hops:


  1    31 ms      32 ms      31 ms      2000:1::1
  2    50 ms      50 ms      63 ms      2001::20
  3    94 ms      94 ms      94 ms      2001:1::20
  4   125 ms     109 ms     125 ms      2000:3::2


Trace complete.
```

Using both IPv4 and IPv6

In this section, we'll see how to make **IPv6-only** hosts communicate with other IPv6-only hosts through **IPv4-only** devices. There are several methods for doing this; we'll discuss IPV6 over IPv4 tunneling using **Generic Routing Encapsulation (GRE)**.

The GRE method **encapsulates** IPv6 packets within IPv4 packets and transports them over the IPv4 network. The receiving device **decapsulates** the packet and sends only the IPv6 information to the host. For this exercise, we'll use the following topology:

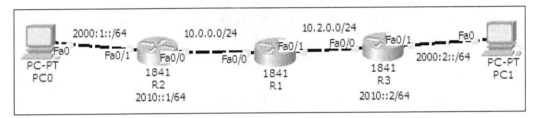

For routing, we will configure EIGRP on IPv4 interfaces for the three routers and static routing on **R2** and **R3**. We will begin by configuring **R1**, which is the IPv4-only router.

```
R1(config)#int fa0/0
R1(config-if)#no shutdown
R1(config-if)#ip add 10.0.0.1 255.255.255.0
R1(config)#int fa0/1
R1(config-if)#no shutdown
R1(config-if)#ip add 10.2.0.1 255.255.255.0
R1(config-)#router eigrp 1
R1(config-router)#network 10.0.0.0
```

Now on the router **R2**, we will configure IPv4 and IPv6 addresses and routing, respectively.

```
R2(config)#ipv6 unicast-routing
R2(config)#int fa0/1
R2(config-if)#no shutdown
R2(config-if)#ipv6 add 2000:1::1/64
R2(config)#router eigrp 1
R2(config-router)#network 10.0.0.0 0.0.0.255
```

Do the same for router **R3**.

```
R3(config)#ipv6 unicast-routing
R3(config)#int fa0/1
R3(config-if)#no shutdown
R3(config-if)#ipv6 add 2000:2::1/64
R3(config)#int fa0/0
R3(config-if)#no shutdown
R3(config-if)#ip add 10.2.0.2 255.255.255.0
```

The only configuration left is the tunnel creation. For router **R2**, carry out the following list of commands:

```
R2(config)#int tunnel 0
R2(config-if)#tunnel source f0/0R2(config-if)#tunnel destination
10.2.0.2
R2(config-if)#tunnel mode ipv6ip
R2(config-if)#ipv6 address 2010::1/64
```

Note that the destination IP is the IPv4 address of interface `f0/0` of **R3**. Configure the other end of the tunnel on router **R3**

```
R3(config)#int tunnel 0
R3(config-if)#tunnel source f0/0
R3(config-if)#tunnel destination 10.0.0.2
R3(config-if)#tunnel mode ipv6ip
R3(config-if)#ipv6 address 2010::2/64
```

The only thing left now is to configure static-IPv6 routes for the prefixes `2000:1::/64` and `2000:2::/64`.

```
R2(config)#ipv6 route 2000:2::/64 2010::2
R3(config)#ipv6 route 2000:1::/64 2010::1
```

Use the simple PDU tool to check connectivity between **PC0** and **PC1**. Use the `tracert` command to find the path that the ICMPv6 protocol takes.

```
PC>tracert 2000:2::2
```

```
Tracing route to 2000:2::2 over a maximum of 30 hops:

1   0 ms        0 ms        0 ms        2000:1::1
2   0 ms        0 ms        0 ms        2010::2
3   0 ms        0 ms        0 ms        2000:2::2
```

```
Trace complete.
```

This shows IPv6 packets going through the tunnel.

Summary

In this chapter, we learned how to use IPv6 with Packet Tracer. We saw how to configure IPv6 static and RIP routing, and also configured IPv6-only hosts to communicate over an IPv4 path by tunneling traffic.

In the next chapter, we'll explore the world of wireless devices and learn how to use the physical workspace to determine the range of those devices.

Setting Up a Wireless Network

9

Wireless networks are growing everywhere; one can find Wi-Fi hotspots at most public places. Packet Tracer has a limited number of wireless devices but provides an unlimited number of possibilities. When configuring a wireless network, one has to consider the physical range of connectivity. Even though it is only a simulator, the physical workspace of Packet Tracer will enable us to test the wireless range of our network using its capability of moving around devices. Towards the end of this chapter, we'll also configure a RADIUS server to provide authentication for our wireless network.

Wireless devices and modules

Packet Tracer provides wireless modules for PCs/laptops and for routers to enable wireless connectivity. Following are the wireless modules:

- **Linksys-WMP300N**: This is available for servers, PCs, and laptops. It provides one 2.4 GHz wireless interface with protocols supporting Ethernet. Once plugged in, this module is configurable through the **PC Wireless** utility available in the **Desktop** tab.

- **PC-HOST-NM-1W**: This is a basic wireless interface that provides one 2.4 GHz wireless interface with support for Ethernet. This module isn't configurable.

- **PC-HOST-NM-1W-A**: This is similar in features to the preceding module, except that it provides a 5 GHz wireless interface.

- **HWIC-AP-AG-B**: This is a router module that works with 1841 and 2811 routers. It functions as an integrated access point and supports single band 802.11b/g or dual band 802.11a/b/g radios.

Now, we will look into the devices; Packet Tracer has wireless end devices as well as access points.

- **TabletPC-PT / PDA-PT / WirelessEndDevice-PT**: These three devices provide the same functionality, they only represent different things. These devices come with a built-in wireless interface.

- **AccessPoint-PT / AccessPoint-PT-A / AccessPoint-PT-N**: These are generic wireless access points with minimal configuration options. All of them have an antenna and a port to connect to a device, such as a router or DHCP server.

- **Linksys-WRT300N**: This wireless device provides a web interface similar to the one provided by a real Linksys model for configuring a **SSID** (**Service Set Identifier**), wireless authentication, WAN port, and much more. This device has 4 Ethernet LAN ports and 1 Ethernet WAN port which can be connected to a router or model that provides internet.

Now that we know the network devices available in Packet Tracer, let's start configuring a wireless network. We will use two access points with two different SSIDs, as shown in the following figure:

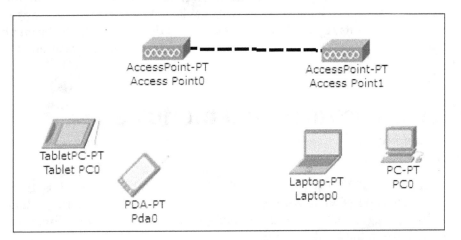

For a change, we will use **TabletPC-PT** and **PDA-PT** as wireless end devices. Once this topology is created, you'll find that these devices pair haphazardly with different access points. So, we will set the **SSID** field of **Access Point0** to Office and that of **Access Point1** to Guest.

Open each access point, go to the **Config** tab, select **Port 1**, and change the **SSID** field, as shown in the following screenshot:

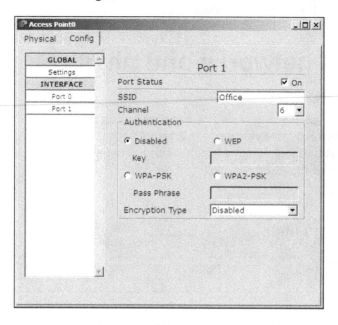

Now open each wireless end device, go to its **Config** tab, choose the **Wireless** option under **INTERFACE**, and change its SSID, as shown in the following screenshot:

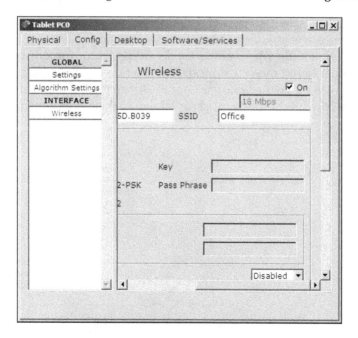

You'll now see wireless lines from each end device connecting to their respective access points. Assign IP addresses to all of them from the same subnet space and use the simple PDU tool to check connectivity.

Wireless networks and physical workspaces

In the real world, each wireless device has a range upto which it can provide wireless connectivity. Packet Tracer simulates this range with the use of physical workspaces. We can see what happens when a laptop with a wireless interface is moved out of wireless range. For this exercise, we'll use the following topology:

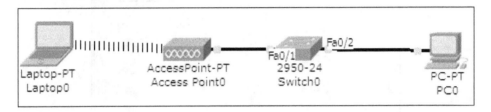

This topology has a wireless access point (**Access Point0**) connected to a switch (**Switch0**), which is connected to a PC (**PC0**). We also have a laptop with a wireless interface.

Configure IP addresses on both the PC and laptop; we'll use IP addresses 10.0.0.1 and 10.0.0.2 respectively. Now ping these devices from one another to test connectivity. Moving to the physical workspace, navigate to **Home City | Corporate Office**. You'll find a round mesh that represents the range of the wireless access point. We are now going to move the laptop to the new office building, out of the wiring closet, and place it in the corporate office, as shown in the following screenshot:

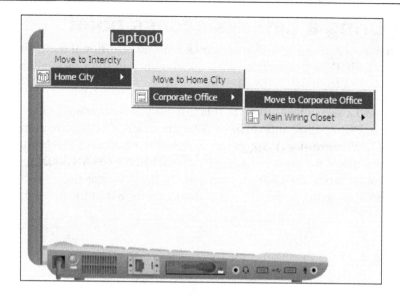

Going back to the corporate office, move the laptop out of this wireless range and test the connectivity by pinging the PC. We will find that this fails because the laptop is out of range, as shown in the following screenshot:

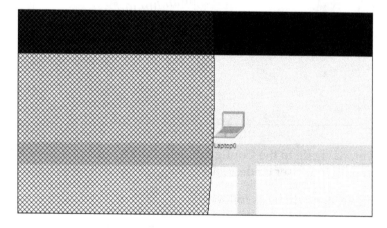

Thus, we've demonstrated the range of wireless devices using the physical workspace.

Configuring a Linksys access point

So far, we have configured wireless networks without additional features such as encryption or DHCP. In this section, we'll use the Linksys devices available in Packet Tracer and create a topology with all these features.

We will also add a server (RADIUS) to this topology and enable RADIUS authentication. **WPA2-PSK enterprise** will be the mode of authentication we will choose in the Linksys router (**Wireless Router0**). After building this topology, switch the default module of the laptop (**Laptop0**) with a **Linksys-WMP300N** module. Open the Linksys router, go to the **GUI** tab, navigate to the **Wireless** tab, and change the **SSID** field. We'll be using Linksys for this demo, as shown in the following figure:

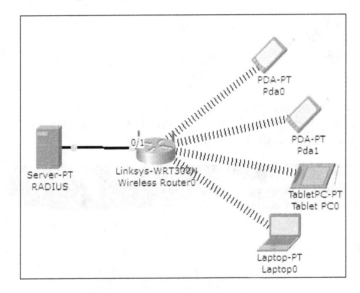

Open the server, navigate to the **Config** tab, select **AAA**, and configure RADIUS authentication with four user credentials. Configuration will be as follows.

Network configuration will be as follows:

ClientName	ClientIP	ServerType	Key
Linksys	192.168.0.1	**Radius**	password

User setup will be as follows:

UserName	Password
alice	pwd
bob	s3ret
john	secr3t
user1	passwd

Configure a static IP for the server as `192.168.0.50`. Next, under the **GUI** tab of the Linksys router, navigate to **Wireless | Wireless security** and enter the following settings:

Security Mode	WPA2 Enterprise
Encryption	**AES**
RADIUS Server	192.168.0.50
RADIUS Port	**1645**
Shared Secret	password

Move on to the wireless end devices, go to the **Config** tab, select **Wireless**, and enter the following settings:

- **SSID**: Linksys
- **Authentication**: WPA2
- **User ID**: john
- **Password**: secr3t

Make sure you use a different pair of credentials for each wireless end device. Once this is configured, the end device will get an IP address and you'll see the wireless link indicating a connection.

Now, we'll configure the laptop that has the Linksys module. Go to the **Desktop** tab, open the **PC Wireless** utility, choose the **Profiles** tab, and click on **New**. Enter any name here, you'll see a list with the SSID name shown, click on **Advanced Setup** and a wizard will guide you through the process.

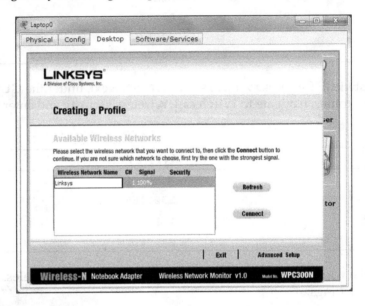

Use the simple PDU tool to test the connectivity. If you use the simulation mode before a wireless connection is established between two devices, you will see the RADIUS packet being sent to the server by the router.

Summary

This chapter introduced you to the wireless devices used in Packet Tracer. We also configured a simple wireless topology without any authentication and used the physical workspace to demonstrate the range of wireless devices. Finally, we mixed technologies such as WPA2, RADIUS, and DHCP and created a topology that uses Linksys devices.

In the next chapter, we'll see how to segment a network at Layer 2 by configuring VLANs, and also see how to configure routing between VLANs.

10
Configuring VLANs and Trunks

A switch breaks up collision domains and is a single broadcast domain. So how about breaking the single broadcast domains into multiple ones? **VLAN (Virtual LAN)** makes this possible and on a single switch we can have multiple broadcast domains. But once you create multiple VLANs on a switch, it becomes tedious to replicate the same configuration on all the other switches. This is where **VTP (VLAN Trunking Protocol)** comes in. So we have multiple switches with different VLANs and VTP, making management easier. But how do we make a device in one VLAN communicate with a device in another VLAN? We'll cover this in InterVLAN routing.

Creating VLANs and VTP domains

VLAN is a technology used to partition a single layer 2 network into multiple broadcast domains. This is done to restrict communication between devices that share the same broadcast medium. However, these devices can communicate with one another through a layer 3 device, such as a router. This is similar to connecting devices to different switches and then connecting them all to a router to separate broadcast traffic.

As more and more VLANs are created, it becomes tedious to replicate the configuration across all switches, which was why VTP was created.

We'll first learn about creating VLAN and assigning ports to it. VLAN 1 is created by default on all switches, and all ports reside in it. This VLAN is called the management VLAN.

To create a VLAN, use the following command:

`Sw1(config)#vlan 2`

The VLAN ID can be between 1 and 1001. The IDs 1002, 1003, 1004, and 1005 are reserved. Once this command has been entered, you are taken to the VLAN subconfiguration mode. This is the place where we can assign a name to the VLAN.

`Sw1(config-vlan)#name finance`

Assigning a name to a VLAN is optional; by default, the name is VLAN0002. Next, we will assign a few ports to this VLAN. To assign many ports to a single VLAN, the `range` command can be used, which then selects multiple interfaces.

`Sw1(config)#interface range f0/10-20`

To assign these ports to VLAN 2, use the following command:

`Sw1(config-if-range)#switchport access vlan 2`

Let's verify if the ports were indeed assigned to the correct VLAN.

`Sw1#show vlan`

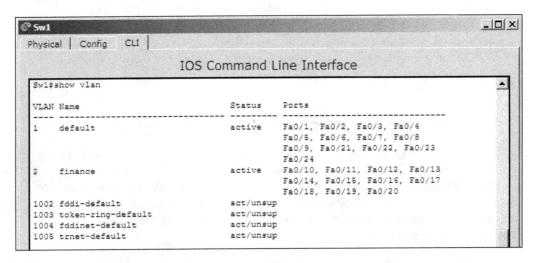

Note that in the above example, some of the output has been omitted for brevity.

We will now create a topology with three switches to demonstrate VTP. VTP has three modes: server, client, and transparent.

- **Server**: This is the default mode of VTP; in this mode, switches are allowed to modify their VLANs and send VTP advertisements.

- **Client**: In this mode, switches listen for VTP advertisements from other server switches. Client switches aren't allowed to modify their VLAN database locally.

- **Transparent**: This mode works independent of other switches. In this mode, the switch only forwards the VTP advertisements it receives and does not generate any, neither does it modify its own VLANs based on the VTP advertisements.

The following topology will be used for demonstration:

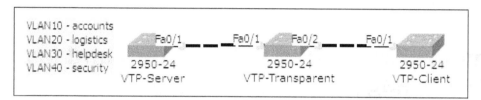

1. In the first switch (**VTP-Server**), we will have four VLANs with different names. Then, we will set all the switch-switch ports to trunking.

   ```
   VTP-Server(config)#interface Fa0/1

   VTP-Server(config-if)#switchport mode trunk

   VTP-Transparent(config)#interface range Fa0/1-2

   VTP-Transparent(config-if-range)#switchport mode trunk

   VTP-Client(config)#interface Fa0/1

   VTP-Client(config-if)#switchport mode trunk
   ```

2. Since VTP is already in server mode, we will just change the VTP domain name and set a password.

   ```
   VTP-Server(config)#vtp domain My-Office

   Changing VTP domain name from NULL to My-Office

   VTP-Server(config)#vtp password s3cRet

   Setting device VLAN database password to s3cRet
   ```

3. Move on to the second switch (**VTP-Transparent**) and make it transparent.

   ```
   VTP-Transparent(config)#vtp mode transparent
   ```

4. The final task is to move the third switch (**VTP-Client**) to client mode.

   ```
   VTP-Client(config)#vtp mode client
   ```

5. You do not have to change the domain of this switch, as changing it to client will make it pick up the domain name from the server. However, it is necessary to set the VTP password.

```
VTP-Client(config)#vtp password s3cRet
```

The configuration is done; now, use the `show vlan` command on the **VTP-Client** switch to see the new VLANs. This example is only to demonstrate VTP. This topology won't allow normal communication between **VTP-Server** and **VTP-Client**, as the switch in the middle (**VTP-Transparent**) doesn't have any of the VLANs we configured.

InterVLAN routing with routers and layer 3 switches

Although VLAN is used to split the broadcast domain, it is necessary to enable communication between two or more VLANs at layer 3 using IP routing. This is called InterVLAN routing and can be configured using both routers and layer 3 switches. This requires allocating a different IP subnet for devices in each VLAN.

We will configure InterVLAN routing by connecting the router to a switch using a single link. All the traffic to other VLANs passes through this link, to the router and back again through this link. This method of configuration is also called **router-on-a-stick**, as a single link to the router handles all traffic.

InterVLAN on a router

We will use the following topology for this setup:

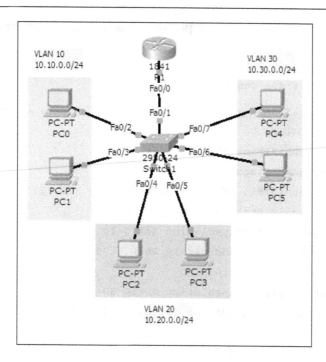

As stated earlier, each VLAN will have IP addresses from different network ranges and the router's interface will have three IP addresses – each belonging to a different network.

1. After IP addresses have been assigned to all PCs, create the necessary VLANs on the switch and assign the ports to them.

    ```
    Sw1(config)#int range f0/2-3
    Sw1(config-if-range)#switchport access vlan 10
    Sw1(config-if-range)#int range f0/4-5
    Sw1(config-if-range)#switchport access vlan 20
    Sw1(config-if-range)#int range f0/6-7
    Sw1(config-if-range)#switchport access vlan 30
    ```

2. Configure the switch port that connects to the router as a trunk link. More on this in the *Switch-to-switch trunk links* section.

    ```
    Sw1(config)#int f0/1
    Sw1(config-if)#switchport mode trunk
    ```

3. Now, moving on to the router portion of the configuration, bring the interface up.

```
R1(config)#int f0/0
R1(config-if)#no shutdown
```

4. We will now create the subinterfaces. Each will have its own IP address in a different network.

```
R1(config-subif)#int f0/0.10
R1(config-subif)#encapsulation dot1Q 10
R1(config-subif)#ip address 10.10.0.1 255.255.255.0
R1(config-subif)#int f0/0.20
R1(config-subif)#encapsulation dot1Q 20
R1(config-subif)#ip address 10.20.0.1 255.255.255.0
R1(config-subif)#int f0/0.30
R1(config-subif)#encapsulation dot1Q 30
R1(config-subif)#ip address 10.30.0.1 255.255.255.0
```

5. Notice the `encapsulation` command here. It specifies the VLAN ID the interface will handle.

6. That's it, now test the connectivity between hosts on different VLANs using simple PDUs or a ping. The first packet will always time out as it takes some time for the **ARP (Address Resolution Protocol)** to complete.

Try using `tracert` to see the path the packet takes.

InterVLAN on a layer 3 switch

The only layer 3 switch present on Packet Tracer is **3560-24PS**. We will use the same topology by replacing only the router with the layer 3 switch, as shown in the following screenshot:

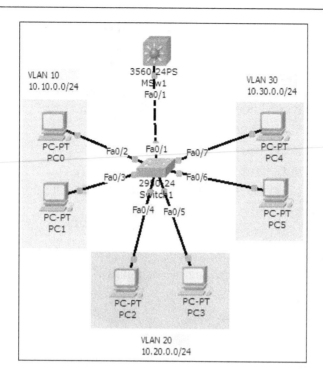

Creation and configuration of VLANs is the same on the layer 2 switch, hence it won't be repeated here. So, we'll move to the layer 3 switch straightaway.

1. Since the switch-switch link on the layer 2 switch was set to trunking mode with the `switchport mode trunk` command, the same port on the layer 3 switch will also be in trunking mode. This can be verified as follows:

   `MSw1#sh interface trunk`

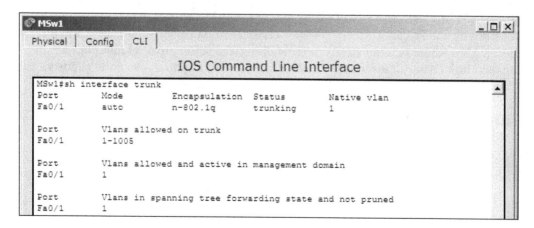

The trunking status indicates this. More on how this port automatically moved to trunk will be discussed in the next section (*Switch-to-switch trunk links*).

2. We will configure what is called **SVI (Switch Virtual Interface)**, which will act as layer 3 interfaces for each VLAN.

```
MSw1(config)#int vlan 10

MSw1(config-if)#ip add 10.10.0.1 255.255.255.0

MSw1(config-if)#int vlan 20

MSw1(config-if)#ip add 10.20.0.1 255.255.255.0

MSw1(config-if)#int vlan 30

MSw1(config-if)#ip add 10.30.0.1 255.255.255.0
```

3. These interfaces will stay down, as this layer 3 switch doesn't have VLANs 10, 20, and 30. So we'll create them as follows:

```
MSw1(config)#vlan 10

MSw1(config-vlan)#vlan 20

MSw1(config-vlan)#vlan 30
```

4. As each command is entered, the associated SVI will come up. IP Routing has to be enabled.

```
MSw1(config)#ip routing
```

5. Use the simple PDU tool to test the connectivity.

Here, too, the first packet will always time out as the ARP process takes some time.

Switch-to-switch trunk links

When two switches are connected together, there must be a mechanism to identify the VLAN a frame belongs to. We aren't talking about the physical layer but about the data link layer. When two switches are connected together, each one needs to know to which VLAN the traffic is destined for. This is where VLAN tagging comes in; when a frame moves over a switch-to-switch link, the source switch tags the frame with the VLAN ID, and this switch-to-switch link is known as a trunk.

Following is a screenshot of an inbound and an outbound PDU, captured in simulation mode, when a PC in VLAN 10 pinged a PC in VLAN 30:

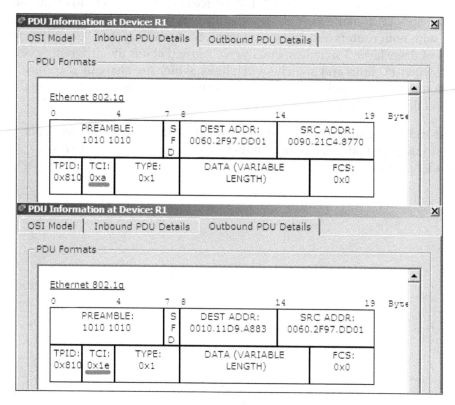

Notice the **TCI** (Tag Control Information) field that contains a hexadecimal value; it denotes the VLAN ID. So, the inbound PDU has **0xa**, which is a VLAN 10 source, and the outbound PDU has **0x1e**, which is a VLAN 30 destination.

Analyzing broadcasts in the simulation mode

The concept of VLAN is to split the broadcast domain: so, in this section, we will see how broadcasts are handled in a VLAN environment using the simulation mode. Use the same InterVLAN topology we used previously. From **PC0** ping to 255.255.255.255, this sets the destination MAC address to FFFF.FFFF.FFFF, which is the layer 2 broadcast address. Switch to the simulation mode and see what happens. The switch receives an ICMP packet from **PC0**, and sends out two copies of it: one to the router and another to **PC1**. If this network weren't divided into VLANs, the ICMP packet would've been sent to each and every PC connected to the switch.

Summary

In this chapter, we learned how to use the devices in Packet Tracer to create VLANs, and to set up VTP to make their management easier. We also configured InterVLAN routing with both routers and layer 3 switches. So, by now, you'd be familiar with the SVIs of these layer 3 switches. Finally, we learned about the differences between normal switch-PC links and switch-switch links, which are also called trunks. The simulation mode of Packet Tracer is of immense help here, as it enables visualizing the packet flow in a VLAN environment.

The next and final chapter will show you how to create practical assessments in Packet Tracer so that you can distribute them and also use them to test your students or interview candidates.

11
Creating Packet Tracer Assessments

We've finally arrived at the final chapter of this book. So far, we've been using Packet Tracer to learn things ourselves, but in this chapter, we will create assessments with Packet Tracer to test how much other people have learned. In addition to being a simulator, Packet Tracer combines the feature of an assessment tool with a lot of potential. Creating an assessment is as easy as creating an initial network or creating an answer network (or rather, a final network).

The Activity Wizard guides you through the creation of an assessment. It is made accessible by navigating to **Extensions | Activity Wizard,** or by pressing *Alt + W*. In this chapter, we'll create a simple assessment with a PC, router, switch, and a server, and configure a simple **Access Control List** (**ACL**).

The welcome screen and instructions

The **Welcome** screen allows you to enter **Author Information** (author name and comments). The **Instructions** section is where you enter questionsand objectives for the user to see. This section uses HTML syntax to format the instructions. A set of supported tags are listed in Packet Tracer's help file.

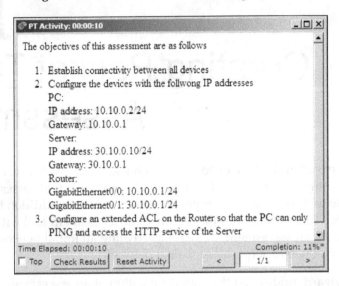

This is an example of using HTML ordered lists with the `<ol>` and `<li>` tags.

The initial network

The following figure is what the examinee will see when the assessment file is opened. Clicking on the **Show Initial Network** option will take you to the logical workspace, from where you'll have to add devices. We will only add the devices shown here, and not connect them or assign IP addresses to them.

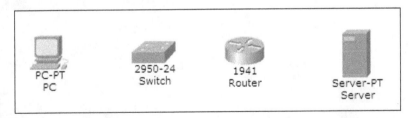

We'll open the **CLI** tab of the router, change the hostname, and set an enabled password by entering the following commands:

```
Router>en
Router#conf t
Router(config)#hostname R1
R1(config)#enable secret cisco
```

We'll stop the creation of the initial network here. Click on the wizard hat and wand icon on the bottom-left corner to return to the wizard. Save this topology by clicking on **Export Initial Network to File**; we'll be using this file on the answer network.

Now, we will choose features that will be locked in the main interface, so that users do not take help from the several tools of Packet Tracer. There are a lot of items to be checked under the **Locking Options** tab. The following screenshot shows the items to be checked under the **Interface** option:

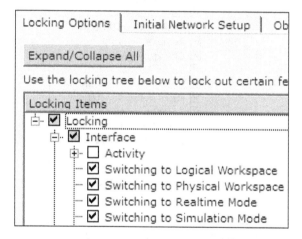

Next, we'll see the items to be selected under the **Topology** option.

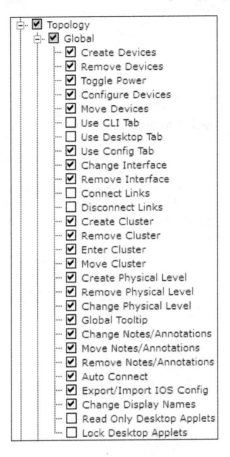

Now, for the **Existing Devices** option, check for the items that need to be selected according to the following screenshot. We'll first see the **PC checklist**:

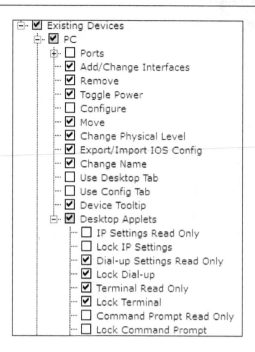

The **Router** option within **End Devices** has the following items checked:

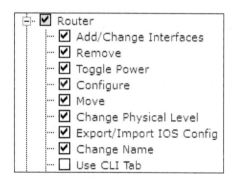

The **Server** option within **End Devices** has the following items selected:

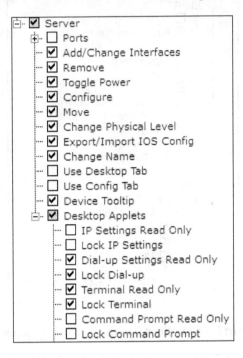

That's all; **Simulation** should now be fully checked.

The answer network

Now let's move on to creating the answer network. Open the **Answer Network** section and import the file that we previously saved. We will now finish this network setup. This is the finished network you'd want the end users to create. Click on **Show Answer Network** and you'll be taken to the logical view with the same four devices again. Our finished network will look like the following figure:

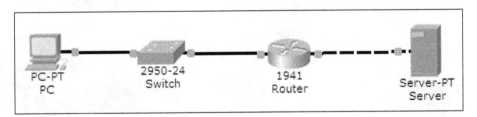

We'll be using the following IP address settings:

- **PC**: The addresses assigned are as follows:
    - ° **IP address**: 10.10.0.2
    - ° **Subnet Mask**: 255.255.255.0
    - ° **Gateway**: 10.10.0.1

- **Router**: The settings configured are as follows:
    - ° **GigabitEthernet0/0**: 10.10.0.1 (Connected to the switch)
    - ° **GigabitEthernet0/1**: 30.10.0.1 (Connected to the server)

- **Server**: The addresses assigned are as follows:
    - ° **IP address**: 30.10.0.10
    - ° **Subnet Mask**: 255.255.255.0
    - ° **Gateway**: 30.10.0.1

After assigning IP addresses to the PC and server, do the same to the router.

```
R1(config)#int g0/0
R1(config-if)#ip add 10.10.0.1 255.255.255.0
R1(config-if)#no shut
R1(config-if)#int g0/1
R1(config-if)#ip add 30.10.0.1 255.255.255.0
R1(config-if)#no shut
```

Now, we'll configure extended ACL on the router so that only **ICMP (Internet Control Message Protocol)** and HTTP traffic is allowed.

```
R1(config)#ip access-list extended 100
R1(config-ext-nacl)#permit icmp any host 30.10.0.10
R1(config-ext-nacl)#permit tcp any host 30.10.0.10 eq www
R1(config)#int g0/0
R1(config-if)#ip access-group 100 in
```

Test if things work correctly by opening the PC and pinging the server. Then try to test the connectivity using the `ftp` command from the PC to the server IP address.

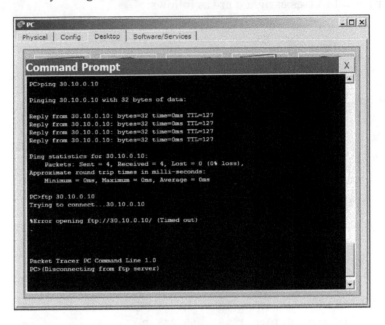

The FTP connection fails as expected (as shown in the previous figure). Now open the **Web Browser** utility and see if the web server is accessible. To incorporate it into our assessment, we need to test the same with PDUs.

- Create a simple PDU to test ICMP. This should succeed.
- Create a complex PDU to test HTTP. This should succeed.
- Create a complex PDU to test FTP. This should fail.

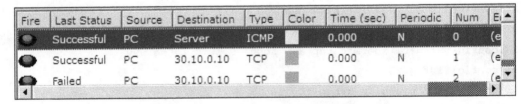

Now that our answer network has been tested (as shown in the previous figure), click on the hat and magic wand icon to get back to the Activity Wizard. Once you are back in the wizard, export this network and save it. We should now select all of the items that will be taken into consideration when evaluating this assessment.

We will evaluate IP addresses of the PC, server, and the router, connections between all devices, and the connectivity between the PC and the server. The following options will be selected under the assessment tree:

- **PC/Server**: We select the following items under this checklist:
  - ° **Default Gateway**
  - ° **Ports**: Select the **FastEthernet0 item, and within that enable the following:**

    IP address

    Port Status

    Subnet Mask

    Link to switch/router: Under this checklist we enable **Type**

- **Router**: We enable the following items in the checklist:
  - ° **ACL**
  - ° **Ports**: Check the following items within the **Ports** option:

    GigabitEthernet0/0: We enable **Access group In, IP Address, Subnet Mask**, and **Type** under the **Link to switch** option

    GigabitEthernet0/1: We enable **IP Address, Subnet Mask**, and **Type** under the **Link to Server** option

After a user has finished configuring all of these items, connectivity has to be checked. Move on to the **Connectivity Test** tab and you'll see the three user-generated PDUs thatwe created. The **Test Condition** field for the first two packets (ICMP and HTTP) should show success, and the third one should show failure. This will be a built-in check to see if the ACLs have been properly configured.

Navigate to the **Settings** tab and set the timer countdown. Setting the countdown will automatically pop up the answer network's window once the time is up. We will set it to 20 minutes.

Click on the **Password** button and set a password. The end users will be prompted for this password if they try to access the activity wizard during the assessment.

Testing the activity

Now that we have prepared our assessment, we should test it and see if it works the way it should. Click on the **Test Activity** button. Complete the assessment and see how the **Completion** percentage information increases. You should also try doing things from the **Locked** list to see how Packet Tracer behaves.

Once you're satisfied with the result, come back to the activity wizard and click on **Save**. The assessment file alone will be saved with a .pka extension. This file can be distributed to anyone who has to take up the assessment. If the end user tries to open the activity wizard, a password prompt will appear.

Summary

This chapter provided you with basic information on creating a Packet Tracer assessment. The assessment engine provides a lot of scope for working with variables. A variable allows flexibility in procuring a wide range of user inputs. Packet Tracer also provides a scripting engine; using your programming skills, you can create more interactivity within the assessment.

Index

T

V

W

Thank you for buying
Packet Tracer Network Simulator

About Packt Publishing

Packt, pronounced 'packed', published its first book "Mastering phpMyAdmin for Effective MySQL Management" in April 2004 and subsequently continued to specialize in publishing highly focused books on specific technologies and solutions.

Our books and publications share the experiences of your fellow IT professionals in adapting and customizing today's systems, applications, and frameworks. Our solution based books give you the knowledge and power to customize the software and technologies you're using to get the job done. Packt books are more specific and less general than the IT books you have seen in the past. Our unique business model allows us to bring you more focused information, giving you more of what you need to know, and less of what you don't.

Packt is a modern, yet unique publishing company, which focuses on producing quality, cutting-edge books for communities of developers, administrators, and newbies alike. For more information, please visit our website: www.packtpub.com.

About Packt Enterprise

In 2010, Packt launched two new brands, Packt Enterprise and Packt Open Source, in order to continue its focus on specialization. This book is part of the Packt Enterprise brand, home to books published on enterprise software – software created by major vendors, including (but not limited to) IBM, Microsoft and Oracle, often for use in other corporations. Its titles will offer information relevant to a range of users of this software, including administrators, developers, architects, and end users.

Writing for Packt

We welcome all inquiries from people who are interested in authoring. Book proposals should be sent to author@packtpub.com. If your book idea is still at an early stage and you would like to discuss it first before writing a formal book proposal, contact us; one of our commissioning editors will get in touch with you.

We're not just looking for published authors; if you have strong technical skills but no writing experience, our experienced editors can help you develop a writing career, or simply get some additional reward for your expertise.

GNS3 Network Simulation Guide

ISBN: 978-1-78216-080-9   Paperback: 154 pages

Acquire a comprehensive knowledge of the GNS3 graphical network simulator, using it to prototype your network without the need for physical routers

1. Develop your knowledge for Cisco certification (CCNA, CCNP, CCIE), using GNS3

2. Install GNS3 successfully on Windows, Linux, or OS X

3. Work your way through easy-to-follow exercises showing you how to simulate your test network using Cisco routers, Ethernet switches, and Virtual PCs

Network Analysis using Wireshark Cookbook

ISBN: 978-1-84951-764-5   Paperback: 276 pages

Over 80 recipes to analyze and troubleshoot network problems using Wireshark

1. Place Wireshark in your network and configure it for effective network analysis

2. Configure capture and display filters to get the required data

3. Use Wireshark's powerful statistical tools to analyze your network and its expert system to pinpoint network problems

BackTrack – Testing Wireless Network Security

ISBN: 978-1-78216-406-7   Paperback: 108 pages

Secure your wireless networks against attacks, hacks, and intruders with this step-by-step guide

1. Make your wireless networks bulletproof

2. Easily secure your network from intruders

3. See how the hackers do it and learn how to defend yourself

SolarWinds Orion Network Performance Monitor

ISBN: 978-1-84968-848-2   Paperback: 336 pages

An essential guide for installing, implementing, and calibrating SolarWinds Orion NPM

1. Master wireless monitoring and the control of wireless access points

2. Learn how to respond quickly and efficiently to network issues with SolarWinds Orion NPM

3. Build impressive reports to effectively visualize issues, solutions, and the overall health of your network

Please check **www.PacktPub.com** for information on our titles

www.ingramcontent.com/pod-product-compliance
Lightning Source LLC
Chambersburg PA
CBHW060151060326
40690CB00018B/4075